*BRANDING IS SEX*

# BRANDING

*IS*

# SEX

*GET YOUR
CUSTOMERS LAID and
SELL THE HELL
OUT OF ANYTHING*

## DEB GABOR

BRANDING IS SEX

*Get Your Customers Laid and*

*Sell the Hell Out of Anything*

ISBN   978-1-61961-427-7   *Print*

978-1-61961-428-4   *Ebook*

LIONCREST
PUBLISHING

*For their obsession with creating kick-ass brands that win, I dedicate this labor of love and passion to the employees, clients, friends, and fans of Sol Marketing.*

# CONTENTS

# INTRODUCTION

**MANY YEARS AGO**, I read a book written by legendary NCAA basketball coach John Wooden. While he was head coach of the UCLA men's basketball team, Wooden earned the nickname "The Wizard of Westwood" for winning 10 NCAA national championships, including a record seven in a row. The part of his book that I still remember to this day was when Coach Wooden explained that he simply could not, not coach basketball. Something compelled him to coach. He never stopped coaching. Wooden reached the pinnacle of sports success and was a national celebrity. But while driving through the neighborhoods of Los Angeles, when he'd see kids shooting hoops with bad form, he'd pull his car over and jump out and coach those unsuspecting kids on hand position and proper form—without a need for anything in return.

That's how I feel about branding. I can't not talk about branding. I can't not write books and give speeches about branding. Branding has been my life's work for the past 25 or so years. So, just like that story about Coach Wooden, when I see kids on the street corner selling unbranded lemonade, I always pull over and lecture them on the importance of branding. Just kidding. Okay, so that's a joke, but I'm deadly serious when I say that companies who manage their brands poorly, or worse yet, don't manage their brands at all, drive me nuts. A company that doesn't pay attention to branding won't be around long. Just ask the leaders of Oldsmobile, Kodak, Polaroid, Circuit City, Borders Books, The Sharper Image, Blockbuster Video, or Pets.com.

I have more than 25 years' experience doing branding for big companies, across industries, markets, geographies, and product types. I've even branded political candidates. Back in 2003, I struck out on my own and started a brand consulting firm called Sol Marketing. Now I get to help all kinds of companies and organizations understand, establish, maintain, promote, and, sometimes, resurrect their brands. Since I started this company, I have developed and standardized a functional methodology that works for companies of all sizes and in all industries, whether they serve consumers or business customers. This book will teach you that methodology.

Just like Coach Wooden, I believe that when you have a gift for something, you have to share it. My destiny is sharing this information with CEOs, CMOs, marketing managers, entrepreneurs, sole proprietors, and leaders in businesses and nonprofits. I feel moved every day to leap out of bed (figuratively) and help propel other people to success in their businesses by understanding and executing brand strategy. I'm happiest behind the scenes helping entrepreneurs, entrepreneurially minded executives, and the leaders of great organizations uncover the ahas that can take their brands to the next level. Branding is my life's work, and the many success stories that my team and I have played an integral part in move me deeply.

Yes, there are other books out there about branding. But, in my opinion, most of those other books that purport to help people understand, make sense of, and do branding are ineffective. They're either very academic or very theoretical and don't actually tell you how to do anything that a real-life business would do. I don't think you need a Ph.D. to do branding. My goal here is to provide a concrete foundation and basic how-to plan—written in plain English—so you can learn everything you need to know about developing and building a brand. And it all starts with uncovering the story of the brand.

This book begins with the underpinnings of brand strategy

and stops at the point where you begin communicating and delivering a brand experience to customers. I want to be really clear that this is not a brand management book. This is not a brand marketing book. This is a book about understanding what branding is, understanding the importance of it, being strategic about it, and learning what you need to know about branding so you can start doing it yourself. If you're an entrepreneur or a small business owner, you're in the right place. If you're a CEO or CMO, this book is for you. Here's the bottom line: if you're in business, you need to understand what's in these pages.

I speak about branding all over the country to groups of marketers, entrepreneurs, business people, and even political candidates. People often say to me, "Yeah, yeah, I get it. I get it. Branding. Yup." Sometimes I get a glimpse into those "Yeah, yeah, I get it" brands and see that their brands are in disarray, decline, or worse. Here's the problem: for most business owners, branding is not intuitive. It's not straightforward and easy to understand like sales or product development or accounting. It's not scientific. It's not quantitative. There are many moving parts and many opportunities for pitfalls along the way. But don't worry, this book simplifies branding and breaks it down for you so you can take these lessons and apply them to your own business. After you read this book, if you still don't get it, never fear, professional help is just a phone call away. My team at Sol Marketing has created millions of dollars in shareholder value through building kick-ass brands. And we'd be happy to do the same for your company should you feel you need us.

## WHO SHOULD READ THIS BOOK

There are two broad groups who should read this book right away: entrepreneurially-minded business leaders and marketers. This book will be especially helpful to leaders at any company that faces deep, existential strategic problems. In other words, problems so serious that the company's very existence is at stake. I'm not talking about superficial problems like, "We need a new logo. We need to make the font on our website bigger. We need more yellow." I'm talking about epic challenges like, "Fierce competitors are coming. We can't keep up. We're losing market share. We're becoming irrelevant. We could lose everything."

I also want to empower marketing leaders within organizations. As marketers, these bright folks understand the value of branding, but their CFOs don't. Often these marketing leaders need leverage to sell an investment in discovering and articulating their brand value. I want this book to be a tool that provides that leverage and supports them in being heroes within their own companies.

So why is there often internal resistance to spending time and money on branding? It's because branding is not intuitive. The engineering, technical, and financial people rely upon numbers. The more quantitatively driven business leaders among us tend to think that branding lives in this netherworld of artsy-fartsy fluff. In many businesses, branding is simply misunderstood. If your company doesn't have a leadership team or managers who came from great brand-focused companies such as Procter & Gamble or Kraft Foods or General Mills or Kimberly-Clark, they probably don't know the full breadth and depth of what the term branding covers. They kind of know what it's about, but they're a little sketchy on the "why" of branding.

Sadly, many people in the C-suite tend to think of branding almost as an afterthought. They consider branding the domain of graphic designers and copywriters. This type of crazy talk makes me sigh deeply, hang my head with worry, and want to down a bottle of Cabernet in one sitting.

Sometimes companies push branding down into the lower levels of the marketing department, mostly because it's misunderstood. I've heard business leaders say, "Branding? That's our logo, our color scheme, our typography, and the kinds of photographs we use." Well... yes. It's all of that. But that's just the part of the iceberg you can see.

## 10 INDICATIONS YOU HAVE A BRANDING PROBLEM

1. Your company's salespeople each use a different "pitch" to potential customers.
2. Your employees can't explain in casual conversation why your company exists or what it does.
3. Your revenues are tanking.
4. "Me too" brands have entered the market and are stealing share.
5. Your desired brand identity (what you think it should be) and image (what customers think you actually are) don't match.
6. You can't answer the question: "What does our customer actually think of us?"
7. You can't answer the question: "How do we elevate our customer's self concept?"
8. You are unable to express a singular benefit your brand provides.
9. You feel a consistent negative "vibe" throughout your entire brand ecosystem.
10. You don't know how your brand gets customers laid.

There is so much more to branding. It goes far deeper than package design, color schemes, websites, and advertising.

The branding that this book is about is all the deep foundational stuff that is under the surface of the water; branding ties directly to business strategy and financial results

(I sometimes refer to this as big "B" Branding.) and that's why it is critically important to every business. But companies often see the practice of branding as squishy. I also think people are afraid of it because it's effing hard.

It may make you furrow your brow and wring your hands; however, the good news is, once you understand it, you'll understand its power to bring important focus and precision to how you operate your business. When you start with the fundamentals, I know you will be able to do it. And with branding, the sooner you get after it, the better.

## THE POWER OF BRANDING

Seattle, Washington-based food media company Allrecipes is a great example of the effect of branding on a company's bottom-line success. When I first started working with the company back in 2007, Allrecipes was *Reader's Digest*'s latest purchase and intended to be the linchpin for its parent company's strategy for online food and entertainment content. Allrecipes was *Reader's Digest*'s hope for becoming a digital brand with the power to reach a whole new demographic and psychographic category of people and to bring that new audience into the aging and shrinking *Reader's Digest* family.

At the time of their acquisition by *Reader's Digest*, Allrecipes was kind of like the Craigslist of recipes. Basically, it was a searchable online warehouse of user-created recipes. It didn't have the slickest user interface, nor was the team very clear on exactly who their target audience was beyond the very high-level description of "home cooks." In fact, the company got its name, Allrecipes, almost by default. The founder took several other recipe sites—Cookierecipe.com, Chickenrecipe.com, Souprecipe.com—and brought them all together, really with no brand strategy at all. It was just like, "Hey, we have these 85,000 user-submitted recipes; we're going to put them into this giant searchable, online database. And, we'll just call it, um... Allrecipes."

If Allrecipes had continued on its way as this gigantic amalgamation of searchable user-created recipes without a strategy to carve out a unique role for a certain type of consumer, Google would have eaten their lunch without them even knowing it. As you know, Google is the homepage of the Internet, and during the early days of our relationship with Allrecipes, Google increasingly became the place at which people began their search for recipes. Allrecipes did not have a clear brand at that time, and Google was a huge danger for them. Additionally, other upstart food media and lifestyle brands such as FoodNetwork.com, Epicurious, and *Real Simple*—each with very clear brand strategies—stepped up their online activities.

Thankfully, Allrecipes hired some very smart people. They worked thoughtfully to define their unique role in the marketplace and made it a primary goal to differentiate the company from other online food and recipe destinations, including Google. The Allrecipes brand eventually became less about the recipes themselves and more about making the users feel accomplished in the kitchen for answering the key question, "What's for dinner Wednesday night?" This branding tapped into the psyche of customers and made them a promise—that they could triumph in the kitchen, no matter what their cooking challenges were—putting them light years ahead of the old Allrecipes.

The big win for today's digital brands is when they create the kind of loyalty in which their sites or apps become part of their users' daily routines. Allrecipes accomplished this because it really understood the story that its customers wanted to create for themselves. By spending time with the users of food and recipe websites and learning about the real problems they were trying to solve, Allrecipes determined that its users were less interested in being able to access hundreds of thousands of recipes online and more concerned with winning everyday kitchen battles such as "kids versus veggies," or "What are three more ways I can combine chicken breasts, broccoli, and rice into a dish everyone will eat?" or answering the question,

"How can I make a meal in 30 minutes or less that everyone at the table will eat?"

For the home cooks among us, you probably know that FoodNetwork.com is about empowering home cooks to "cook like a celebrity." Epicurious, the online home of *Gourmet Magazine* and *Bon Appetit*, is about awarding self-described passionate "foodies" with a badge of honor for cooking gourmet meals using special ingredients and advanced techniques. However, understanding its customers' behaviors, attitudes, goals, and desires made Allrecipes singular in its focus to empower home cooks to prepare delicious, palate-pleasing, *everyday* meals. That focus enabled the company to align all of its business strategies—from the products it developed and launched, to the advertisers it courted for sponsorship—with that goal. Today, there's still no other site that is laser-focused on answering the simple question, "What's for dinner Wednesday night?"

So what was the result of this deep branding work? Allrecipes skyrocketed from being about half the size of the category leader, FoodNetwork.com, to become the number one recipe site on the Internet. And remember, FoodNetwork.com also has a popular cable TV channel to promote its brand. But through the power of branding, Allrecipes prevailed. It took about two-and-a-half years of hard work, but it paid off. The company's rebranding created tremendous stakeholder value, and Allrecipes eventually sold at a valuation nearly three times its purchase price.

We'll dive deeper into the Allrecipes brand success story in coming chapters. And you'll read a fascinating interview with the former Allrecipes CEO. But the point of this story is that branding can make or break a company. Branding can have a huge positive impact on the bottom line, and it can build tremendous financial value. On the flip side, branding done poorly—or not done at all—can literally destroy a company, cause financial value to decline, and lead a company into intense competition where profits are competed away. In other words, the stakes could not be higher.

## A WORD ABOUT THE TITLE, *BRANDING IS SEX*

You might be wondering exactly how branding is like sex. I will explain this in detail in chapter five rather than here in the introduction, because to appreciate this concept fully, you'll need to understand some of the key principles in chapters one through four. But I'll summarize the concept quickly so you're not entirely in the dark.

Strong brands help their customers solve problems, present a positive image to the world, feel empowered, feel accomplished, and feel like the hero in their own personal stories. Think about what happens when you're feeling like you're on top of the world, feeling heroic, and feeling that everything is working out the way you hoped it would. No matter which cliché you use—the feeling of having wind in your sails, the world on a string, or holding life by the balls—that feeling puts you in the mood for sex.

All branding is about making people feel so good through the use of your brand that they want to take a roll in the hay. It really is. It's not only about feeling sexy, it's also about having sex. When the story you tell yourself through the brands you choose truly makes you feel heroic, you're feeling your power, and you're in the mood to get laid.

When I say "having sex," it may mean literally jumping into bed naked with your partner. But it may also have a more figurative meaning: experiencing the exhilaration of neighbors or other moms in the carpool complimenting, fawning over, and praising you, as well as having your ego stroked and receiving appreciative feedback from your husband and your children. All of these things feel great, too. This concept of branding as sex will become increasingly clear by the time we reach chapter five.

Branding is a big topic, and there is a lot to cover. So let's get started. Modern business is more competitive than ever, and if you hesitate, another strong brand could sneak in and seduce your customers into bed. Like Coach Wooden famously said, "If you don't have time to do it right, when will you have time to do it over?"

# ONE

# BRAND OR BE BRANDED

**"**

*If you do not define your brand and what you stand for in the marketplace, someone else will—usually other companies or consumers or socially connected journalists or bloggers or pundits. You do not want anyone else branding you.*

JODI KAHN, CHIEF CONSUMER OFFICER, FRESHDIRECT.COM

Business leaders and marketers ask me all the time, "When should we brand?" My answer is always the same, "Early, often, and always. You can never stop branding." This is one of the reasons I am so passionate about my job leading a brand consulting firm. Branding is so much more than just a logo and a color scheme. Branding is the sum total of all of your relationships, emotional connections, and promises you make to your customers. Branding happens in 360 degrees and at all touch points. Your customers define your brand, but you own it. You control the identity; your customers control the image. If you don't control it yourself, your brand will take on a life of its own. What happens when a company isn't branding early, often, and always? What happens if you let the universe take ownership of your brand? Most likely disaster.

Branding is not optional, it's essential. And it should be continuous. You should always be thinking about it and working on it. Otherwise, very bad things can happen. Your customers can lose touch with your brand and leave you. A competitor with a strong commitment to branding can overtake you. Or, perhaps worst of all, the market will define your brand for you. Brand yourself, or someone else will brand you. It's *very* dangerous if you let the market, or your customers, or the news media, or bloggers, or social media, or your competitors define your brand for you. Let me illustrate this with a couple of examples.

One classic example is the entire cable TV industry. Cable television companies are similar to public utility companies in many ways, because for decades they essentially had no competition. They owned a local "franchise," which allowed them to do business in a particular geographic area, and they were exempt from competition. So if you wanted to watch more than the three local over-the-airwaves broadcast stations, you had to order cable and pay a monthly fee. In other words, the regional cable companies had mini-monopolies because their customers had few options for home entertainment. As a result, they often didn't treat their customers well. The cable companies knew their customers weren't going to leave. As a result, poor customer service became an ingrained way of doing business.

I don't know if you've ever personally had the experience of being a customer of any of the big cable TV companies. If you have, then you probably experienced an overwhelming sense of dread whenever you had to call the cable company for something. Maybe you called with a billing question, or perhaps you needed a technician to come out and repair something at your house. Dealing with cable companies is not a pleasant experience.

Invariably, you'll wait on hold for 30 minutes. When you do get a customer service rep on the line, you have to repeat all your account information you've already entered via the interactive voice response system. Then the rep asks you a bunch of stupid questions you already answered for the previous person. When you do schedule your appointment, customer service provides you a four-hour window of time when you need to be home. The technician shows up either early or late, or not at all. If your window is 12:00 p.m. to 4:00 p.m., you'll get a call at 3:59 p.m. The technician will say he's running late and then show up at 4:30 p.m. Then you get your cable bill, which is already too high to begin with, and discover that the company charged you way more than you expected for the service call. When it comes to customer satisfaction—or the lack of it—it doesn't get much worse than this.

With that atrocious level of customer service, some of the big cable companies earned a dismal reputation among customers, and their brands took a hit. You can go into a party and overhear people talking about how frustrated they are with their cable provider. "Oh gosh, I had to call the cable company the other day. What a nightmare. I'm still upset!" Everybody in the room utters a sigh of disgust because they've experienced the same thing.

Pretty soon, some company such as Consumer Reports or Temkin Group releases a survey and finds that the cable industry has the lowest customer satisfaction scores of any industry. Then the news media picks up the story. The bloggers start ranting. Twitter goes crazy. And before you know it, the cable industry has been branded as an awful industry that abuses its customers. It can be very difficult to shed that reputation, and it can take years.

This story is an example of the title of this chapter, "Brand or Be Branded." The cable industry lost control of its brand and let someone else—in this case, customers—own the brand. When you don't take control of your brand's image, and you don't properly manage the relationship you have with your customers, the results can be devastating. And they show up on the bottom line.

Cable TV companies eventually did have to learn to compete. Aggressive competitors moved in: Dish Network and DIRECTV, as well as over-the-top home entertainment providers such as Netflix, Hulu, Amazon Prime, and others. Now the cable companies are learning the hard way that their reputation for poor customer service could cost them dearly.

## IRRATIONAL LOYALTY IS THE GOAL OF BRANDING

The antithesis of the cable company is any business that treats its customers so well that those customers develop irrational loyalty to that brand. My relationship with Zappos.com is an example of this in practice. Zappos's entire brand is a customer experience. Zappos has successfully branded a particular type of customer service and customer *love*, and it shows in everything they do: from the free overnight shipping and free returns they offer, to their exceptional, over-the-top telephone customer support when the unfortunate happens. As a result of my experiences with the Zappos brand, I am so irrationally loyal to Zappos that if they sold chicken feed and I had chickens, I would have to buy it from them. This is the type of customer relationship that all brands should aspire to. You'll learn more about why I'm so obsessed with Zappos in chapter six.

Let's explore that notion of irrational loyalty a bit more. When I consult with clients, they often ask me to illustrate the importance of branding. That's when I like to talk about irrational loyalty—this notion of being loyal to something no matter what. The idea behind irrational loyalty is that you have so much positive juju built up in your emotional bank account for a brand and you are so into it that you would go back and buy from the company no matter what it did to you. If you're irrationally loyal to a certain product or company, it's as if it could disappoint you, and you would still remain a loyal customer.

A great example of a product that inspires irrational loyalty is the Apple iPhone. I've owned every model of iPhone since the beginning of iPhones. I've had iPhones that heated up in my hand and burned the side of my head when I tried to talk on them. I have broken half a dozen iPhone screens, which I think are too delicate. And the iPhone costs around $600! For a phone!

I believe there are more durable, technologically superior, better-functioning products out there. But I don't care. I won't switch to a different brand because I'm irrationally loyal to the iPhone. I once looked at a gorgeous Samsung phone with a big beautiful screen. I caressed it in my hands and lusted after it. But after about a minute of pure animalistic attraction to the sexy device, I ran out of the store because I felt like I was *cheating* on Apple. Sad, I know. But *that* is the definition of irrational loyalty. Later in this book, you'll read about a bar and grill chain with such loyal customers that they tattoo its logo somewhere on their bodies. That's loyalty.

The concept of irrational customer loyalty embodies some key lessons about the importance of branding. Irrationally loyal customers say things such as, "I love the whole experience," or "I like how it makes me feel," or "I like what that brand says about me." The best-loved brands in the world are the ones that become *part* of the person who uses them. What does it say about the person that he or she uses this brand and what does it say about you that you use this brand? That is a key question that we'll explore in detail later in the book.

The reason I don't use a Samsung phone is because I don't want anyone to see me using a Samsung phone. I like what it says about me that I'm an iPhone user. I don't care if there are other products that cost less and function better. I like the iPhone. I am obsessed with Zappos, even though I have to wait for my shoes to arrive with the UPS man. I know there's a perfectly good Nordstrom store with thousands of pairs of shoes just a few miles from my house. I can walk in there, buy a pair of shoes, and wear them home today. It seems crazy that I'd trade instant gratification for a customer experience in which I feel loved and embraced, doesn't it? But I still prefer to shop at Zappos because I like what it says to the rest of the world and to myself about who I am as a person.

Branding is so much more than a clever logo, pretty colors, or a funny advertising campaign. Branding is about building strong emotional connections with customers. That's a seriously smart business move that will have an enormous impact on growth and profitability.

We'll talk more about emotional connections later in this book. But consider this: one of the most significant emotional connections humans experience is love. When people talk about the brands they're loyal to and the brands they engage with, they often use the word "love." I love Apple. I love Zappos. I love Audi. I used to drive a Volkswagen, but sorry Volkswagen, I never loved you.

## BRANDING IS EMOTIONAL

Branding is highly emotional. For instance, I am a dedicated wearer of these odd-looking running shoes from a brand called Hoka One One. They are the ugliest, most cartoonish-looking shoes in the world. The colors are so hideous and gaudy; I assume the designer must be color-blind. They really look silly. But I am irrationally loyal to these shoes because of how good they feel on my feet and the story they tell about me as an athlete.

I'm so loyal to this brand that every 500 miles or so I buy myself a new pair, because that's what Hoka says I should do. When they feel this good, the uglier the better! And as I've grown in fondness for my clunky Hoka One One Cliftons and noticed other runners wearing them, I began to love that they are clearly recognizable and they say something about me. These shoes scream, "I don't care how silly I look, I'm a self-confident runner, and I do what's best for my body and my health."

They don't say that I am a fool for spending $130 every six months to buy a new pair of hideous-looking running shoes that give me Frankenstein feet. What they say about me is that I care about body alignment. I care about foot-fall, and, as a recreational fitness person, I actually care about the impact of running on my body. They say that I won't wear just any old running shoe that's on sale; I value health and performance over price, and I *deserve* to wear the world's most technologically advanced "zero-drop" running shoe. My love affair with Hoka One One has ascended to the point that I would never consider wearing another brand, not even in the privacy of my own home gym. Between you and me, once after a few drinks, I flirted with some Adidas and Asics, but I'm in a dedicated, monogamous relationship with my Hokas.

That's because of the relationship I have with the Hoka One One brand. My wearing of Hoka shoes both elevates my self concept and expresses something about me to the rest of the world. The best brands in the world are the ones that say something about their users. In other words, branding is about how a product or service contributes to the story you are creating for your own life and how you articulate that to other people.

Here's another example. Let's say you're driving in your car, and I pull up next to you at a stop sign. I'm driving a Ford

F-150 truck. You look over and do a double take when you see this middle-aged woman in the driver's seat of a huge F-150 truck. You're there in your Toyota Corolla, and here I am in this beast of a vehicle. So, based upon my choice of vehicle, what do you know about me as a human? Probably not that much beyond what you can piece together from what I look like, what I'm wearing, what I'm driving, and perhaps what I'm drinking. Based upon my Ford F-150, you can probably deduce that I'm tough. I'm dependable. I'm practical. I probably haul a lot of stuff around. Style and fuel efficiency are not as important to me as being seen as somebody who is legitimate in my chosen line of work. I value American-made automobiles, and perhaps I enjoy driving "the" quintessential pickup truck of our time. The details you've noticed about me from just seeing me in the driver's seat of that F-150 truck are all part of my personal story. Those details don't only tell you a story about me, they become part of the story I tell me about myself.

## BRANDING STARTS WITH UNDERSTANDING YOUR CUSTOMERS

This will be a common thread throughout this entire book: branding doesn't come from the *company*, branding comes from the *customers*. Your brand lives in your customers' needs and desires, as well as their perceptions of their connections to you. Branding is not an inside-out activity; it's an outside-in activity.

The branding methodology I explain in this book comes down to getting inside your customers' heads and then working inward from there. What do your customers think? How do they behave? What do they need? Where do they go to get it? Where do they shop? How much are they going to spend? What's important to them? How does it make them feel? And how does it advance the goals that they have for their own lives? This is where branding starts.

## FRESHDIRECT—FASTER FROM THE FARM TO THE FORK

FreshDirect is an online grocery store on the East Coast. When you order from FreshDirect, you can place a grocery order online today and receive delivery at your home or office the next day. Since FreshDirect began operations in 2002, the company has featured a large selection of popular national brands, as well as their own private-label products. The company has direct relationships with regional growers and producers to ensure that the food you get is the best-tasting, healthiest, and most nourishing product available. For example, their in-house bakery and partnerships with local farms, fishermen, and meat purveyors provide food that's several days fresher than what you'll find in most grocery stores. In addition to traditional grocery items, they sell household products, bulk goods, and a variety of convenience items, such as prepared meals and partially prepared items that make cooking and eating a breeze.

But as you may be aware, the world has undergone a seismic shift since 2002. The food procurement space is changing rapidly. When I say food procurement, I'm talking about how people get the food they eat. This space is becoming increasingly crowded every year, if not every month. It seems like new startup food delivery companies are popping up faster than you can say, "Fifth-floor walk-up." So, how does an established player like Fresh-Direct compete with energetic, innovative, tech-savvy, and, often, extremely well-funded competitors? Let's dig into this case study.

I started working with FreshDirect in 2013. At that time, they viewed their competitors as traditional brick-and-mortar grocery stores such as Whole Foods Market, Gristedes, and Safeway. Many of those traditional stores were beginning their forays into home delivery with their own homegrown services and strategic partnerships, such as Peapod. It was about that time that several delivery companies not attached directly to the grocers—such as Instacart and Max Delivery, which both deliver groceries in an hour or less—began to offer other methods for consumers to get food delivered right to their front doors almost as soon as they realized they were hungry. Even

Amazon got into the act with their AmazonFresh business. With these new consumer choices, FreshDirect's reality changed in almost an instant.

Nearly overnight, FreshDirect found itself in competition with *dozens* of methods of procuring food and literally *hundreds* of competitors, including other supermarket chains, the neighborhood farmers' market, corner convenience stores, the deli down the street, hundreds of restaurants that deliver, and multiple restaurant delivery services, such as Seamless, GrubHub, and Just Eat. It doesn't stop there; the food delivery business continues to evolve rapidly. Even upstart transportation brand Uber has stepped into the market with their UberEATS offering, in which Uber drivers cruise around the city with 30 hot, ready-to-go meals in the backseat. To New Yorkers, it might seem that every time they come home there are three more flyers promoting a new food delivery option taped to their doors. Further underscoring this trend was the infusion of more than a *billion dollars* of venture capital and private equity funding in food tech companies in 2015 alone.

The methods for procuring food currently available to city dwellers are numerous, diverse, and vastly different from FreshDirect. Luckily, FreshDirect has an enlightened, brand-focused management team. The company's managers are very advanced in their thinking about branding and competitive positioning. Seeing the competitive landscape change before their eyes, they realized, if FreshDirect is just about the procurement of food, and people can get food almost the instant that they're hungry, consumers won't want to wait until the next day to get groceries delivered. Customers are hungry now. So the company started looking at opportunities to play a more meaningful role in its customers' relationships with food. With the Sol Marketing team's help, management asked themselves one of those deep existential questions I mentioned in the introduction, "How do we extend our value beyond just the procurement of food?"

Before making any significant changes to its branding, FreshDirect spent a lot of time and effort really learning every aspect of their customers' relationships with food to assess opportunities to address more of customers' food challenges. In response to all the new competitors, FreshDirect delved into understanding everything it could about consumers' food "life cycles" from the moment they feel hungry, to the moment they think about getting food, to actually getting that food into their mouths. Diving into this research gave FreshDirect management an expanded view of who their competition is and how to position their brand to be about more than just next-day grocery delivery.

These new insights have enabled FreshDirect to expand its view of who its customers are, what its customers are trying to achieve, and how it can succeed in conquering its customers' food challenges. This information now empowers them with strategic opportunities to compete against Seamless, GrubHub, UberEATS, Instacart, Safeway, and all of the other click-and-deliver grocery and food providers.

So after talking to its customers and surveying the competitive landscape, FreshDirect expanded its view of the role it plays in its customers' lives. It isn't just about being a supermarket that delivers. It's about being part of customers' entire food life cycle. As a result, the company's branding has evolved with consumer needs, expectations, and the changing types of relationships that consumers want to have with these kinds of providers.

I can't speak specifically about what changes FreshDirect will make in its branding and business model going forward because I'm the company's brand consultant and those are confidential business strategies. But the point I want to get across is that the competitors challenging FreshDirect now only recently came up on the company's radar. The way the company responded was by doing a deep dive into the lives of its customers to learn as much as possible about every aspect of food procurement and consumption. Remember how I said "brand or be branded" and that your brand comes from your customers, not the other way around? FreshDirect fully embraces that notion, and that's going to propel it to great success. For more information about FreshDirect's experience in building its brand, see the interview with Jodi Kahn, FreshDirect's chief consumer officer, at the end of this chapter. She'll give you more details.

## DON'T KNOW WHAT YOUR CUSTOMERS THINK? ASK THEM!

Most companies don't have a six-figure budget for market research. So how do you learn about your customers? Lo and behold, you learn who your customers are by actually finding and having a conversation with them. Those conversations can take place through informal market research, such as chatting with customers in Starbucks, or through formal research methods, which could include everything from focus groups, to quantitative studies, to depth interviews, to observing your customers "in the wild" through ethnography.

In the case of FreshDirect, we actually followed people around while they shopped. We observed the entire food procurement life cycle. We even used video cameras and asked customers to show us what it looks like in their houses during the dinner hour. They showed us what it was like to shop in traditional grocery stores. They showed us what the insides of their refrigerators and pantries looked like. In some cases, they even showed us the family dog.

Fresh Direct, for all intents and purposes, is an e-commerce company. It has a database full of customer information that it can use to garner insights into how those customers behave. The company looks at buying trends, web analytics, and quantitative analysis and then fills in the data points that are lacking by actually going out and having conversations with customers through informal and formal research. That's how you get customer input. It doesn't matter the size of your company. These tools are available to all.

Even a company that has only four employees and makes $250,000 a year has enough customers to conduct meaningful research. Companies of all sizes, go out and ask your customers about their needs. Probe into how their needs are not currently being met. Ask them, "When their needs are not met, to whom or where do they turn?" Here's a pro tip: smart companies don't just ask this of their own customers; they ask their competitors' customers too.

Customers must always be a central part of the equation when you're doing brand strategy. Unfortunately, there are many agencies out there that believe they can do branding in a black box without talking to customers. To do branding in a vacuum without putting the customers' point of view front and center is a massive mistake. In building a strong brand that connects deeply with customers, you must conduct discovery to gain understanding of customers' needs and the trends, forces, and brands that compete for their attention. The goal is not only to safeguard against what other brands are doing but also to gain insight into your company's unique role in the marketplace and your unique relevance to your ideal customers. In further chapters in this book, we'll talk about all of this. I'll show you how to identify and create a detailed profile of your ideal customer and how to learn everything about him or her and what that customer is trying to achieve in his or her life. And then I'll explain how you make your brand become part of that customer's self concept and the story he or she will tell.

## WHAT ABOUT BUSINESS-TO-BUSINESS BRANDS?

Sometimes business-to-business brands push back on the idea of branding for their products and services. Earlier I used examples about an online retailer, running shoes, the iPhone, the cable company, and a Ford truck. Admittedly, these are consumer-oriented examples. Now, B2B marketers tend to believe that branding only applies to consumer products. They say things like, "Building an emotional connection to an enterprise software brand is impossible. No one cares what story a software platform tells about them."

Well, that's pure bunk. Regardless of what kind of product you're selling and to whom you're selling it, people buy things from people. And every person has a self concept and a personal story that he or she is trying to tell to him or herself and the world. If you're the guy at Dell who makes decisions about the kind of processors you're going to put into a laptop, you're still a human being. So what buying that product says about the person who buys it is still extremely important.

Let's say a purchasing manager at some mid-cap manufacturing company decides to buy Oracle enterprise resource planning software. He cares very much what that purchase decision says about him to his colleagues, his bosses, the executives in the C-suite, and his end users. And he wants that purchase of Oracle software to elevate his self concept. See, he still desires some emotional relationship with Oracle. He is looking to create the story of his career and his professionalism, his technical prowess, and business smarts. This guy's purchase of Oracle software really is part of the story he wants to tell about himself. So, branding is just as important in the B2B world as it is in consumer-facing products and services. We'll get into the how of this in the coming chapters. Just remember to always keep the customer at the center of all of your conversations about brand strategy.

We have a lot to talk about in this book, including the key strategic underpinnings of branding. One is the notion of the three big questions you must answer about your brand, which we'll explain in detail in chapters three, four, and five. The other one is the brand values pyramid, which we'll explore in the next chapter. But first, check out this interview with Jodi Kahn from FreshDirect.

 **INTERVIEW**

**WITH JODI KAHN, CHIEF CONSUMER OFFICER, FRESHDIRECT.COM**

Jodi is a client I admire. She represents the ultimate in using customer insights to ensure that brands remain relevant and competitive. I've worked with her on many brands, including *Reader's Digest*, Allrecipes, Taste of Home, NBC Universal, Patient Channel, Newborn Channel, and, currently, FreshDirect.

**Why is branding important?**
Your business is your brand and your brand is your business. Businesses that are going to be enduring have to spend time nurturing, building, and refining their brand.

**What would you say to a business owner or an entrepreneur who hasn't thought much about branding?**

I would say stop and spend some time with it. Spend some time thinking about companies that you admire. Try to understand how that brand has helped them build the business scale that they want. Ask yourself how you get at a consumer's heart. I believe your business proposition will not be fully formed unless you include your brand proposition.

**If a company doesn't brand actively, then they run the risk of the marketplace or competitors branding them. Do you agree?**

Yes. As a business, it's your right to tell your story. If you do not define your brand and what you stand for in the marketplace, someone else will—usually other companies or consumers or socially connected journalists or bloggers or pundits. You do not want anyone else branding you.

**How do you think about branding at FreshDirect?**

We believe our business is our brand and our brand is our business. But we started as a supply chain and logistics company. Branding came later, as an important step once we got to know who our customers were. And that's what Deb really helped us with. We took a pause and said we need to get to know our customers. Once we understood what our customers thought of us, then we identified the gap between what they thought and what we define our brand as. We went on a mission to close that gap and tell our story differently. This helped us connect in a real relevant way with how consumers shop for food, how they eat, and how they think about food in their lives. The brand became bigger than just the service.

The brand of FreshDirect is about being connected to your food life, and we bring you the freshest in food and solutions to let you live the life that you want. That's very different than being an online food delivery company.

**How do you get to know your customers?**
Certainly, in today's age we have a lot of access to information about consumers and their perspectives. In this digital age, everyone writes an online review. We pay attention to that. But to truly understand your customers, you need to talk to them, and you need to watch them shop. It really opens up insights that allow you to understand why your customers are your customers. That's so crucial to building the business.

**You said, "Watch them shop." How do you do that?**
You can invite customers into a conference room and give them wine and pizza and ask them to shop online. You can do that informally. So, if you are on a bootstrap budget, you could literally just have a wine and pizza party and ask people to come in, set them up with some laptops, and ask them to shop.

**What kind of things are you observing at that time?**
You give somebody a task and say, "I want you to find a recipe and then go buy the ingredients," and you see how they do it. You would

invite somebody that's married with kids versus single, suburbanites versus urban dwellers, and you see how they shop differently.

**You can just sit right there in the room with them and keep it casual?**
Absolutely. Yes.

**What if you don't have a big budget for customer research? How can somebody learn about his or her customers with no budget or a boot-strap budget?**
You do a slice of it. You work with a research company to understand if you can't spend $100,000, what can you do for $20,000? You must have a profile of your customers or your intended customers because that's who you're building your business for. Understanding basic consumer profiling is going to be money well spent. You'll waste less time and less money if you know the target you're going after and you understand their motivation and their drivers.

**How do you keep your brand relevant going forward? Is it an ongoing process?**
You are always branding. At FreshDirect, I'd say we always need to be in the food conversation. We need to be relevant. If it's going to snow on Saturday, the brand of FreshDirect needs to know that it's going to snow and suggest maybe you need XYZ for your food basket. But seeing and understanding where consumers are at and what their life moments are and being relevant to the way that consumers want to see themselves is an every day, every-hour activity. It's very, very important to know what your brand is and what it isn't.

What's the company that your brand wants to keep? What are the news outlets you want your brand to be in or not be in? So that is an every-hour exercise.

**What has been most helpful to you in branding FreshDirect?**
I think that Deb's formula is precise and very thoughtful. Deb has deep experience in helping companies face reality and find brands that open territory that can build businesses. I certainly have been the beneficiary of Deb's expertise and brainpower because she has done this with me in four or five different businesses. Small businesses and big businesses, she really does run the gamut. She's consumer obsessed. She lets the truth of the consumer speak, and she's really pretty direct about it.

# TWO

# THE BRAND VALUES PYRAMID

**"**

*Every single business has a brand associated with it. Whether the business owner thinks about brand or not, a brand does exist. They may not be managing that brand, they may not really be articulating that brand, but a brand exists. And if a business owner isn't clear about what their brand stands for anymore, they can simply ask their customers and their customers will tell them.*

LISA SHARPLES, CEO, FEXY MEDIA

49

As we all learned in Marketing 101 class in college, product marketing begins with understanding what the customer needs and then creating a product, pricing it correctly, and putting it in all the locations where a customer wants to buy it to fill that need. In school, marketing professors taught us that customers make rational purchase decisions. However, as a student of branding and marketing over the past 25 or so years, I've learned that reason informs, but emotion persuades. Branding is really the practice of meeting customers' needs—functional and emotional—in their entirety. The practice of branding requires digging a lot deeper into your customers' needs, wants, and desires and then trying to uncover the inner stories customers tell themselves. Marketing 101 was a good start, but to really understand branding, we need to leave the business school and walk across campus to the psychology department.

## MASLOW WAS A MARKETER

If you think back to Psychology 101 class in college, you probably remember studying Maslow's hierarchy of needs. Maslow shaped his hierarchy like a pyramid, with the most basic human needs—food, water, shelter, air—at the base and loftier, more emotional needs at the top. The theory is that all humans must first solve for the lower levels of the pyramid before moving to the upper levels.

Maslow's Hierarchy of **NEEDS**

SELF-ACTUALIZATION — Morality, Creativity, Spontaneity, Problem solving, Lack of prejudice, Acceptance of facts

ESTEEM — Self esteem, Confidence, Achievement, Respect of others, Respect by others

LOVE & BELONGING — Friendship, Family, Sexual intimacy

SAFETY — Security of body, of employment, of resources, of morality, of the family, of health, of property

PHYSIOLOGICAL — Food, water, sex, sleep, biological functions

Once a person is no longer worried about finding food and water, he or she can move up to solve the problem of safety. Once that person figures out safety, he or she can move up to love, and so on.

What many people don't realize is that Maslow was actually a marketer. He created his hierarchy of needs to help explain human motivation. It turns out that his pyramid of needs is also a brilliant analogy for branding. It's a useful construct for being able to create the core DNA of a brand and then articulate that in the marketplace.

Just as Maslow's hierarchy explains human motivation, the brand values pyramid illustrates the idea that when they make a decision to purchase or use a brand, people are motivated to achieve certain needs. After fulfilling one need, a person seeks to fulfill the next one, and so on. The basic, functional needs that a brand must meet are at the bottom: what a brand offers and does. Brands must meet even more of their customers' emotional needs as customers move up the pyramid. And once a brand ascends to the top of the brand values pyramid, it supports customers' process of becoming self-actualized.

Let me explain with an example. I always like to use the example of automobiles because it's really easy for people to understand. Think about all of the various brands of automobiles that you know. You could probably name off the top of your head 25 or 30 brands and models of automobiles, right? The things that make all of those products you named "automobiles" are what we call baseline requirements, which equate to the base of Maslow's hierarchy. In Maslow's pyramid, those basic physiological needs are food, water, shelter, air, and so on. In automobiles, the baseline requirements are wheels, an engine, and a steering wheel, as well as seats, mirrors, windows, and the basic functional benefit of getting you from point A to point B. All cars must meet these baseline requirements and deliver these functional benefits, or today's consumer auto-purchase market will not take them seriously.

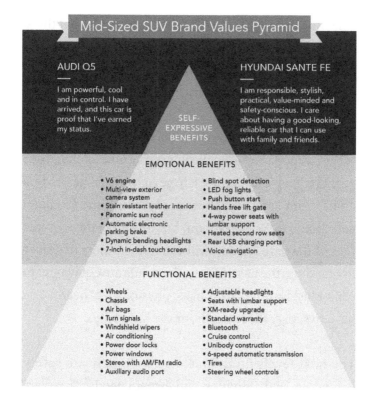

## Mid-Sized SUV Brand Values Pyramid

**AUDI Q5**

I am powerful, cool and in control. I have arrived, and this car is proof that I've earned my status.

**SELF-EXPRESSIVE BENEFITS**

**HYUNDAI SANTE FE**

I am responsible, stylish, practical, value-minded and safety-conscious. I care about having a good-looking, reliable car that I can use with family and friends.

**EMOTIONAL BENEFITS**

- V6 engine
- Multi-view exterior camera system
- Stain resistant leather interior
- Panoramic sun roof
- Automatic electronic parking brake
- Dynamic bending headlights
- 7-inch in-dash touch screen

- Blind spot detection
- LED fog lights
- Push button start
- Hands free lift gate
- 4-way power seats with lumbar support
- Heated second row seats
- Rear USB charging ports
- Voice navigation

**FUNCTIONAL BENEFITS**

- Wheels
- Chassis
- Air bags
- Turn signals
- Windshield wipers
- Air conditioning
- Power door locks
- Power windows
- Stereo with AM/FM radio
- Auxiliary audio port

- Adjustable headlights
- Seats with lumbar support
- XM-ready upgrade
- Standard warranty
- Bluetooth
- Cruise control
- Unibody construction
- 6-speed automatic transmission
- Tires
- Steering wheel controls

## BRANDING LESSONS FROM MY GARAGE

Currently, I have two cars parked in my garage. I drive this sweet midsize Audi SUV, and my daughter drives a midsize Hyundai SUV. From the outside, they look very similar. They're about the same size, and they have many of the same features. They have four wheels, windows, a steering wheel, an engine, four doors, side-view mirrors, and so on. They also each have cargo space, some off-road capabilities, and all the creature comforts we've come to expect in our midsize SUVs. The basic things that these two cars have in common with one another that make them function are the baseline requirements for anything in the midsize SUV category.

When we think about baseline requirements for any brand in the category, those are the things that absolutely have to be there. That's the ante just to get into the game—to be a "that" in any category. Those are *not* the things you build your brand on or market on, but those are the features that, if they are absent, will cause customers to defect. In branding, the baseline requirements are equivalent to what Maslow refers to as basic physiological needs. You have to satisfy those needs, or the brand dies.

The next levels up in Maslow's hierarchy are safety, belonging, and affiliation and esteem needs. These are the benefits that make you feel like you're part of a group and protected. In the brand values pyramid, these middle tiers describe how certain features make you *feel*. In branding, we refer to these as emotional benefits. In the car example, these emotional benefits come from features that make you feel safe, secure, confident, cool, smart, and a variety of other feelings. In car talk, these are the "options." Emotional benefits can provide a competitive advantage, but they are not your brand.

## Today's Options Are Tomorrow's Standard Equipment

Here's a lesson for you. I'm old enough to have purchased a car that didn't have power door locks and power windows. Believe it or don't, there was a time that car buyers paid extra for these options. However, one car brand (and I honestly can't remember which it was) started making power door locks and power windows standard on all their models. And then the other brands followed suit, which made these options standard equipment for the entire category. The lesson in this is that it's tempting to try to differentiate your brand based upon bells and whistles alone. Who doesn't think it's easier to market awesome features such as self-parking capabilities and massaging seats? But brander, beware. As soon as someone else in the marketplace imitates those options and consumers come to expect them as baseline requirements for anything in the category, they become standard equipment.

The options packages in the middle of the pyramid for today's cars are things such as Bluetooth; voice-activated, in-dash navigation; heated seats; self-darkening mirrors; bi-xenon headlamps; and a variety of other cool things. Not every model of car in a category offers those features, so they're still somewhat differentiating and can command a premium purchase price. However, these features are easy for other brands to imitate, so they don't define the brand, and certainly aren't sustainable long-term brand differentiators.

In-dash navigation makes me smile. It makes me feel confident I can reach my destination without looking like a complete idiot with clients in the car. It provides solid emotional benefits that enhance the quality of my driving experience. But up until a few short years ago, in-dash navigation was rare and available only on the most exclusive luxury automobiles. Today, Hyundai (and Honda and Toyota and Chevrolet and Ford, and the other usual suspects) offers it as an option. I predict that in a few short years, in-dash navigation will go the way of power door locks and power windows (and antilock brakes and power steering) and become expected baseline requirements.

But like the functional benefits we discussed before, emotional benefits alone will never be enough to create and sustain a brand. As smart business leaders and marketers, we expect that customers make rational decisions about the brands, services, and products they buy. But that isn't really the case.

## MIDDLE OF THE PYRAMID FEATURES

To give another example, let's consider running shoes. There are some basic product features that every running shoe must have for the market to take them seriously. Then there are some additional features that only some running shoes have, such as speed laces. The benefit associated with that is you don't have to spend a lot of time lacing, relacing, and tying your shoes. You can get in and out of your shoes quickly. Clever, right?

Sure. But that's a feature that shows up on many running shoes now, so it's a middle of the pyramid type of feature. That feature is something that's easy for someone else to imitate. If you remember just a page or so ago, I got up on my soapbox about the idea that today's options packages are tomorrow's standard equipment. As soon as somebody else offers it, it becomes standard equipment. Differentiating yourself just on the basis of things other people can imitate does not give you a sustainable brand advantage. Don't waste your time doing that.

A duplicable feature can be *part* of your brand story, along with everything else that is unique to your company. If it's a feature that must be there because you have to put a check mark next to it and say, "Customers won't consider us to be relevant in this category without this," then, yes, it needs to be part of the brand story. But is it the lead?

No, it's not the lead of the story.

But you can build a brand on the unique combination of your features, the things you do and you enable your customers to do, plus the things you make your customers feel, and the stories that your brand tells about its customers. The sum total of all of those things is the brand story. When done well, it's impossible for competitors to copy. This is how you build a lasting brand.

## THE IMPORTANCE OF SELF-EXPRESSIVE BENEFITS

Brands, as symbols of a customer's self concept, benefit them in a very profound way by giving them a vehicle to express themselves. Self-expressive benefits—the stuff at the top of the brand values pyramid—enable customers to complete the statement, "When I eat/drink/drive/wear/use this brand, I am ___." When brands provide self-expressive benefits to their users, they can engender deep emotional connections. Consider the difference between the self-expressive benefits associated with Heineken beer, which may heighten a person's self concept of being a sophisticated, discerning, worldly person, with those of Budweiser.

Back to the two cars in my garage: the Hyundai and the Audi both meet the baseline requirements for midsize

SUVs and provide some similar and compelling middle of the pyramid features and emotional benefits. These two cars are so similar in their physical makeup, features, and benefits, that if you were to take the brand names away, they'd be virtually indistinguishable. But everyone can agree that an Audi is an Audi, and a Hyundai is *not* an Audi; it's a Hyundai. Each of these two brands is unique and singular in what they let their owners say about themselves. For me, driving an Audi makes me feel powerful, cool, and in control, while driving the Hyundai makes my daughter feel responsible, stylish, practical, and safety conscious. Those feelings connect us to each of the two brands in very powerful ways. These feelings elevate our concepts of ourselves and support us in telling a story to the rest of the world.

Brands that do really, really well are the ones that say something about their user. The key to successful branding is to make self-expressive benefits part of the brand value proposition to add richness and depth to the brand and the experience of owning and using the brand.

## BRAND STORYTELLING VERSUS CREATING THE STORY OF YOUR BRAND

I want to make sure people understand the difference between brand storytelling and creating the story of your brand. "Brand storytelling" is marketing's hot buzz phrase.

There are many people out there talking and writing about the idea of brand storytelling. Brand storytelling—or telling the authentic story of your brand to *other people*—is how your brand articulates itself through marketing, advertising, social media, PR, and actively telling stories through media and personal interactions. It's the day-to-day management and execution of the brand message through the sharing of a narrative about the brand. Brand storytelling covers things such as the commercials you run, the imagery you use, the videos you put on YouTube, the user stories you share, your blog posts, tweets, and Facebook updates. All that stuff happens at the ground level and flows from the decisions you make in *creating* the story of your brand. To be clear, brand storytelling is very different from what we've been discussing. I'm talking about creating the brand story—which happens at the 30,000-foot level. The methodology I'm talking about in this book is for developing the story that your brand tells the world *about the user*. Once you've settled the story of your brand, then you begin executing—part of which is engaging in brand storytelling.

That's really, really important. The next section of this book is about creating that story. How do you figure out what that story should be? It starts with understanding your customers. Remember, branding is less about the brand and more about the person who uses it. The best brands in the world say something about their users and actually become part of the user's self concept. But that requires you to understand the story your customers are trying to create for themselves through the use of your brand. How do you become part of that story and how do you make them the protagonist? We'll dig into that in chapter five.

## DON'T FOCUS ON FEATURES

Many brands, in the automobile industry especially, tend to market based on middle of the pyramid kinds of features—cool options, the bells and whistles. Just watch any sporting event on television, and you'll see the car commercials. General Motors loves to promote its OnStar communication system. Lexus touts its self-parking function. Mercedes-Benz has amazing magic fingers-style massaging seats.

But since these car ads focus on features, consumers often cannot differentiate one vehicle brand from the other. The next day you can't remember what you saw—it's a blur of shiny dashboards and LED dials. When commercials focus on features, it's hard to tell a Nissan from a Toyota from a Honda.

However, Jeep is an incredible brand that tells a unique story about its users in a way that other SUVs in the

category—such as the Nissan Pathfinder—do not. If some-body drives a Jeep, you know that he or she an explorer, an adventurer, and loves going to new places. The Jeep owner wants to explore his or her surroundings and values rug-gedness. The person who owns a Jeep is a pioneer, whereas some of the other brands tell a much less compelling story, which is basically, "Our SUV is a cheaper imitation of Jeep."

Going back to the brand values pyramid, the top of the pyramid is the stuff that no one else can imitate. It consists of all the things about your brand that make it special, singular, and unique. For example, no other brand of SUV has the heritage and history of Jeep. And Jeep branding reminds customers of that all the time. Just check out the Jeep.com website. Seriously, pull it up right now. The big banner at the top of the page says, "75 years of history. A lifetime of freedom in a world of adventure." That's top of the pyramid stuff. Not bad. No mention, by the way, of antilock brakes, heated seats, or gas shocks. Those are features: middle of the pyramid stuff.

## TELLING CUSTOMERS YOU'RE DIFFERENT IS NOT ENOUGH

In business and especially the startup world, you hear all the time that your product or service must be different from what's already out there. But when it comes to branding, just touting product differentiation won't work—because you're still just talking about features. It is not enough to brand yourself based on what you do differently or better or faster or cheaper than anybody else does, because those are things that other companies can imitate. As soon as they see you out there in the marketplace doing it and customers gravitating toward you, they're going to start doing it too. Since there's more than one way to skin a cat, maybe competitors won't imitate your exact functionality or product features. They will, however, imitate the benefits those features can provide to customers.

That is just the nature of what happens in markets. It's the swarm mentality. Soon your differentiating feature is no longer different. All the brand capital you've built up promoting how you're different is wasted. You'll have to start over building your brand on something else. Ouch.

It's simply not sustainable to market just based on that differentiation. The brands that win are the ones that create an enduring story and bond with customers in a truly emotional way; they make themselves indispensable to their customers. And this is not just for consumer brands. This is also true for business-to-business brands, as discussed in chapter one.

## GET PROFESSIONAL HELP IF YOU NEED IT

People have told me a few times over the years that I need professional help. But that's a story for a different book, maybe for my personal memoir. In this book, let's stick to branding, shall we?

Okay, I'll cool it on the jokes for a while. I'm just trying to lighten the mood because I know we've talked about many weighty concepts here, and your head might be spinning. In this digital age, more and more marketing managers come from an analytical background. I do too. I'm a numbers gal. I'm a very analytical person and all this talk about brands bonding with people emotionally and the inner stories customers tell themselves was hard for me to get my mind around at first. This is not how we data junkies typically think. But after I really began to understand it, and actually see it with my own eyes, it became second nature to me.

Maybe you're thinking right now, "This stuff is hard. I don't feel like this is something I can do." Have faith. I believe in you. You can do this. Start by finishing this entire book. Read the chapters and all the interviews. At the end, if you don't grasp the fundamentals—if it's all still a big blur—don't worry. You can always bring in a professional. I've built my entire company on helping businesses master their own brand strategy. This stuff isn't easy. And the stakes are huge. Companies that hire Sol Marketing have a big, hairy brand strategy problem they need to solve before it's too late. So even if you decide to bring in professional branding help, by having read this book a few times, you'll be in a better position to work effectively with the consultant and understand his or her strategies.

The painful truth is, when you hire a brand strategy consultant such as Sol Marketing, you have to be prepared to face difficult facts. You have to be willing to hear stuff that maybe hurts a little, that shows you've been doing it wrong. And you have to be willing to hunker down, go the distance, and make some tough decisions about what you're not going to do anymore.

As I stated earlier, branding is an existential problem. You really don't have a choice. If you want your brand to thrive, you need to do the exercises in this book. If you don't, then someone else is going to come over and lure your customers into bed. Then you'll spend all your resources fighting for share, instead of getting really close to your ideal customers who will bond with you for life in a highly irrational way.

Early-stage startups don't need to spend a lot of money on this right now. But they definitely need to go through the exercises and then have some high-level discussions about the brand so everyone is on the same page. The point where you need to bring in an expert is usually when you've stalled out. I would say my best clients are mid-cap companies in growth mode. I love companies that are between $100 million and $1 billion in revenues who are trying to get to the next level. They seem to benefit the most from having outside professional help.

 **INTERVIEW**

WITH LISA SHARPLES, CEO, FEXY MEDIA, FEXY.COM

Lisa Sharples is the former CEO of Allrecipes and the current CEO of Fexy Media.

She is the model CEO for embracing the importance of branding early, often, and always. Fexy Media raised a fund to buy niche digital media properties in focused passion areas, such as food targeted at millennials.

## What is Fexy Media?

Fexy Media is a roll-up in the digital media space, and what that means is we are going out and acquiring companies that are very similar but have their own distinct business models and approach their consumers in their own unique way. We're acquiring established brands in the digital media space that are focused on the millennial generation, with a specific emphasis on food. We've acquired some brands maybe you have never heard of and then other brands that are well-known in the space, like SeriousEats.com. As we put these brands together, we're building a national sales team that can sell advertising across all our media properties and platforms. But beyond sales, each brand within the Fexy portfolio operates on their own in their own distinct way. We have acquired each business because it is a great company, and we believe in what the brand is doing for consumers. Our goal is simply to invest more in each brand so they can continue to grow. Two of our food specific brands, SeriousEats.com and Roadfood, are both premier brands with individual teams that have been leading the charge for years. We want to invest resources to introduce these brands to more and more millennials and continue to acquire new brands that offer great content for the millennial generation. We want to deliver media to that generation in a new and very different way with a singular focus on digital.

## Where did you learn about branding?

I went to Kellogg Business School at Northwestern University and majored in marketing. I am definitely a disciple of many of the marketing thought leaders from Kellogg, and I went there specifically to understand branding and marketing.

**Why is branding important?**

Branding sets the strategy for everything. Typically, I'm walking into a company that has an established brand that they're already marketing. I try to understand the brand from the very core: "What does this brand stand for?" I've worked at big companies like Silicon Graphics and Sun Microsystems. I've also had the role of CEO at smaller companies that have been turnarounds. Brand becomes extremely important when you're trying to turn around a company. Sometimes people lose their way and forget what their brand stands for, and you have to go back to the very beginning.

I think branding is at the core of business strategy. You must always start with brand. Even for startups, I think whether or not the founders realize it, they've thought about brand from the very beginning. Answering the question, "Why are you starting this company?" leads to a brand discussion. It's at the very core of why an individual is an entrepreneur and what is motivating them to start this company.

**What are some common mistakes you see people make?**

A lot of entrepreneurs come to me and they say they have an idea. "I'm thinking of starting a company." I ask them the most basic questions, "What problem are you trying to solve? Why do you want to start this company? What's motivating you? What gets you excited every day to walk in and go to work? What is that problem that you're trying to solve for the consumer?" In the technology industry, a lot of people have great product ideas but they don't really know the answer to what problem they're trying to solve. They become enamored with the technology they have created and now they're looking for how that technology can solve problems. You can certainly start a business that way, but the most compelling businesses are the businesses that have started because someone saw a problem in the marketplace and became determined to solve that problem.

**Can you tell us about your branding experience at Allrecipes?**
Allrecipes was a 10-year-old company when I joined as the CEO. The team had obviously built a great brand before I got there because they had eight million unique visitors going to the website each and every month. However, when I first got to the company, I asked the executive team a simple question, "What is Allrecipes?" I individually asked each of my direct reports, "What is Allrecipes to you?" I had about eight different direct reports at the time, and I got eight different answers. For me, it was kind of an aha moment.

**So there was no clear understanding of the brand?**
This happens a lot with fast-growing companies. The team is working so hard and moving so fast to keep up with their growth that they don't really stop and sit down and talk to each other about what they are trying to do. "What is the core problem in the marketplace that we're trying to solve?" Bad things can happen if you don't stop and have those critical conversations as a team on a regular basis. For example, one thing that can happen is everybody sort of decides on their own, in their own respective roles, what problem the company is trying to solve. So you get this mentality, pervasive throughout the company, of really trying to solve all problems for all people because

everybody in their own respective role is trying to solve something a little bit different. This results in a watered-down brand approach because you're trying to be all things to all people, and you end up being nothing special to anyone.

**Why did you bring in a brand consultant?**
At Allrecipes, I brought in Deb and the team at Sol Marketing to help us do what I called a "brand audit" and really get us back to the essence of the Allrecipes brand. We may not have been clear on what the brand stood for, but the eight million people visiting the site regularly knew the value. We needed to ask them why they loved Allrecipes. Then we needed to figure out what we were going to be loud and proud about and what we were going to leave up to other competitors in the space. We needed a go-forward strategy so we could tell our audience and the advertising community that we represented. Conversely, we needed to get a bit cockier in the marketplace and begin to say, "While we understand that's an important part of the digital food space, that's not us." I think that was the big leap we took during our brand audit, and it worked. It catapulted the Allrecipes brand to the next level.

**Did Allrecipes see tangible results after this rebranding?**
When I got to Allrecipes, we were about 40 percent smaller than FoodNetwork.com. I said to my team, "Why aren't we number one?" They all said, "How can we ever be number one? We don't own a cable channel." I took it on as a personal challenge. I didn't just want to be number one because I'm competitive; I wanted to be number one because I wanted to prove to my team that it can be done. About two-

and-a-half years into my tenure, Allrecipes.com eclipsed FoodNetwork.com as the number one digital food site. And still today, Allrecipes.com is larger than FoodNetwork.com. I think there was a lot of great work from the entire team that went into our success, but I do see the brand work we did as a very critical piece.

**Can you talk specifically about the Allrecipes brand?**
Our branding work enabled us to say confidently, "Okay guys, this is what our brand is about. We are about helping the head of household deliver a great meal on a Wednesday night. We're not about fancy dishes; we're not about special occasions; we're about what's on the table for dinner on a Wednesday night. Everything we're doing needs to be working toward that goal and anything that we're doing that isn't working toward that goal, we need to stop doing." With that kind of brand clarity and focus, we were able to drive a lot of growth and stop doing a lot of things that were peripheral to our core brand. Deb believes that getting the customer laid is the ultimate goal of every brand. I interpret what she is saying to mean that your brand gives your customer confidence and wind in their sails. Because of your brand, the customer feels they can accomplish more! She's right.

We wanted the Allrecipes brand to give each and every visitor to the site renewed self confidence and excitement and pride to take that next step; to take that next cooking risk. That is what we continually discussed as a team. Allrecipes is about helping our members succeed in their everyday cooking goals. Whether that's as simple as opening a can of soup and heating it on the stove, or making a complicated dish they'd never attempted from scratch. We want those people to feel empowered and be successful. Because we know that success begets success. If each individual can get a taste of success, they will feel empowered and it will lead to them trying more and taking bigger risks. How do we make sure the customer feels like they can be successful? How can this brand help them with that?

**The food space is highly competitive. How did you differentiate Allrecipes?**

At the time, a lot of the other brands in the food media space were very upscale, and they were talking down as an authority to you as the consumer. Through their language and through their photography, they were intimidating. You would look at a photograph of a dish and you'd think to yourself, "I could never cook anything that will look that perfect." When you looked at your final product and you referred back to that photograph, you were disappointed in yourself. Your internal monologue sounds something like this, "Well, yeah, it came out okay and it tastes good, but it doesn't look right." We had endless conversations about photography: "It has to look real. If this doesn't look like something you could accomplish on a Wednesday night in your house, we should not use the image." We avoided using food stylists and high-end photography for exactly this reason, because all that production made the food seem unattainable. And it was! We would tell our editorial team that they were not allowed to use photographs that had garnishes, because no one puts a garnish on a Wednesday night meal at home. It was these little things that you don't really think about, but it's hard to open up a food magazine and not see garnishes. These little things lead to a feeling that a recipe is unattainable, and the picture makes you feel like a failure, even if you followed the recipe perfectly. We felt that our attention to these details differentiated our brand from a lot of the other food media brands out there.

**Do you have any advice for companies that don't think about their branding?**

Every single business has a brand associated with it. Whether the business owner thinks about brand or not, a brand does exist. They may not be managing that brand, they may not really be articulating that brand, but a brand exists. And if a business owner isn't clear about what their brand stands for anymore, they can simply ask their customers and their customers will tell them.

**Can business owners do branding on their own?**

When I speak to business owners, whether the business has been around for one month or 50 years, I always recommend that they hire an outside consultant and do a brand audit. I think as business owners, we are way too close to our brands. I'd only been at Allrecipes for about six months when Deb came on board to help us with our brand audit, yet I already knew I was too close to the brand. Having someone come in from the outside to help you really understand what your brand means to your consumer is the only way you're going to get a real, unbiased opinion. It's hard to do internally. I always try to encourage people to use outside experts to help them really understand and define their brands.

# THREE

# WHAT DOES IT SAY ABOUT THE CUSTOMER?

"

*If your product isn't branded in a way that "makes sense" to the customer, it won't sell. If it doesn't sell, don't blame the customer for just not "getting it." Blame yourself.*

CHRIS TURNER, STAMPEDE CONSULTING

In the first two chapters, we talked about *why* branding is so important, and we introduced the brand values pyramid. Now we're going to dig into *how* to create your brand's story. In the next three chapters, we'll examine three questions that every brand must be able to answer. The three questions are as follows:

- What does your brand say about your customers?
- What is the singular thing your brand delivers that customers can't get from anyone else?
- How do you make your customer a hero in the story of his or her own life?

In this chapter, we'll examine the first question, which is about the self-expressive benefits we talked about during the explanation of the brand values pyramid.

The first question asks, what does it say about a person that he or she uses this brand? What does it communicate both to the outside world and to the customer him or herself? Answering this question requires you to really get inside your customers' heads and understand what they want to achieve in their lives, how they measure their success in achieving those goals, what they care most deeply about, and, ultimately, how the brand must deliver. These are the questions we'll explore in this chapter.

The second question asks about singularity and indispensability. What is the singular thing that a person using this brand gets from it that they can't get from any other brand? This is one of the hardest questions to answer. We'll explore this topic in chapter four.

And the third question acknowledges that everybody wants to be the hero in his or her own story. Everybody wants to be the protagonist. How does your brand make the customer a hero? If you can answer this, you'll have loyal customers for life. We'll explain this question in chapter five.

At a very high level, everything we do in branding is about answering those three questions. You can take those three questions and almost overlay them on the brand values pyramid. If you do nothing else as a result of reading this book, just try to answer those three questions about your brand. When I consult with clients, if they look like they're overwhelmed or they look like they're not buying it, I say, "Well, let's just answer these three questions about your business." Once we start the process, they see how answering the questions starts them on the path to defining their brand strategy.

## WHAT DOES YOUR BRAND SAY ABOUT YOUR CUSTOMERS?

What does it say about your customer that he or she uses,

wears, drives, eats, or drinks your brand? Earlier in the book, we talked about how the best brands in the world bond in a really strong, emotional way with their customers and become part of their customers' self concept. That self concept is not just the image they project to the world; it's also how they feel about themselves. Think of the customers' stories as their own brand.

That story customers tell themselves equates to self actualization, which is at the top of Maslow's hierarchy of needs. So this is where we really start to identify the top of that brand values pyramid, the self-expressive benefits, and how a brand becomes part of a person's concept of being cool, smart, beautiful, confident, and so on.

What does it say about me that I drive an Audi? In *my* mind it says, "I'm a successful CEO of a business that I founded and that I've built. I'm proud of my accomplishments. I value performance, style and elegance, and I'm willing and able to pay a premium for what I want. But even though I like nice things, I didn't buy a BMW because I don't drive like an asshole." I'm sorry if I offended you if you drive a BMW. But that's the story I tell the world—and myself—by driving an Audi. The Audi helps elevate the concept I have of myself as smart, successful, accomplished, and deserving.

Even very similar products, such as other German-engineered premium automobiles, can have very different brand stories. I drove a Mercedes-Benz for years before I switched over to Audi. Why the change? Because all of a sudden I felt like my dad. I said to myself, "Whoa, I am not a 74-year-old male lawyer from Cincinnati." That Mercedes-Benz, even with its massaging seats, programmable seat positions, and headlights that turn with the curve of the road, expressed something about me that was no longer relevant.

## BRANDING IS NOT JUST FOR LUXURY GOODS

Does that mean that only high-priced, luxury brands tell effective stories about their customers? Absolutely not. Every brand tells a story about its users. An example would be the automobile company Kia. Back when I first started doing brand consulting in 2002, Kia was the example I frequently used to discuss a brand that was just bottom-of-the barrel cheap. Plagued by consistent off-the-assembly-line failures and massive recalls, Kia had earned a reputation as a crappy, Korean-made cheapie that was appropriate for only the least discerning, most-price-conscious drivers who were trying to get from point A to B. Buyers of Kia cars in the early 2000s bought the brand to elevate their self concept of being frugal, utilitarian, and practical.

But fast forward to today. Today's Kia brand is still very affordable. It's still a good value in terms of the features it offers for the price. But along the way, Kia rebranded itself. It created a new story that says its customers are smart, savvy, cool, connected, hip, and young, not that they're cheap. The Kia brand held on to the attributes of being value-priced and practical, but transformed itself to project a completely evolved self concept for its users. Kia is not a luxury brand by any stretch of the imagination, but no one considers it a cheapie either.

Walmart is not a luxury brand either, but it is a very strong brand indeed. It is very clear what Walmart as a retailer says about the people who shop there. It's that, above all, they always value getting the lowest price. It's right there in the store chain's slogan: *Lowest Prices, Always*. What the Walmart brand says about its customers is that they don't screw around with price comparison; they don't shop around. Walmart built its entire brand around that idea, down to the stripped-down, in-store brand experience. Branding is definitely not just for high-end luxury brands. Creating an emotional bond with customers by figuring out what the brand says about those customers is essential for every brand.

McDonald's is another strong brand that offers a low-priced product. Branding does not equal luxury. Branding does not equal high prices. Branding equals putting your customers at the center of your strategy and creating an experience based upon those customers. It requires you to be really intimate with your customers and understand their needs and the stories they want to tell about themselves.

## HOW DO YOU LEARN ABOUT YOUR CUSTOMERS?

How do you learn everything about your customers? Three words: talk to them.

There are many different ways to talk to your customers. On the super-low-budget end of the spectrum, you can just hang around in a Starbucks and ask people to try your product or service and then ask them for their opinions. Be sure to ask open-ended questions, such as: "What do you like about this brand?" Or, "How do you see this fitting into your life?" Or, "What would you change about this?" Actually talking to customers face to face is one of the most valuable things you can do to understand your brand.

Another easy way for marketing managers and executives to interact with customers is by fielding customer service calls or inbound sales calls. Even at the CEO level, if you take customer service calls for a few hours every month, it might just be the most valuable time you ever spend.

The callers won't have any idea you're the CEO, so they won't sugarcoat how they feel about your brand. And you can ask them almost anything you want and they'll answer honestly.

Another free method is hosting a pizza and beer party—or pizza and wine party as Jodi Kahn from FreshDirect described—depending upon your target demographic. Invite friends and friends of friends to visit your office or your home and try your product. Tell them you'll provide take-out food and beverages in exchange for their time. The key here is to make sure you're getting honest feedback. Friends and family usually will try to tell you they love it, even if they don't. So offer them the booze in exchange for brutal, unvarnished honesty.

These three ways of talking to customers are free. Entrepreneurs in early-stage startups and companies without market research budgets should take full advantage of all of these and devise other methods that put them front and center with customers. On the opposite end of the cost spectrum is formal market research, such as in-depth interviews, ethnographies, focus groups, and surveys. Professional focus groups can yield a tremendous amount of data, but they're costly. Many books discuss techniques in market research. If you're on a budget, or you have no budget, you may want to check out the book titled *The*

*Lean Startup* by Eric Ries, which suggests many methods for obtaining customer feedback throughout the development and growth process.

If you are having trouble answering the question, "What does it say about a person that they use your brand?" You need to go out and talk to customers. Ask them directly, "What do you think it says about you that you use this brand?" It's as basic as that. Start there and then you can expand your customer research to learn other important things about your products, services, and brand.

## THE BRAND GRAVEYARD

When I was a senior in high school, my parents bought twin Oldsmobile 98s. They were big, heavy, gas-guzzling, four-door sedans. My brother and I jokingly called them "the living room on wheels" because they had these plush velour seats and squishy, floaty suspensions. They were horrible to drive, to be honest. The purchase of these two cars made my dad "King of the Suburbs," the undisputed ruler of the neighborhood. He didn't just have one of these beasts. He had two of them sitting in the driveway in front of our house. He was so proud and the envy of the neighbors.

Now, mind you, my brother and I were sharing the Plymouth Horizon TC3 UAV (urban assault vehicle) roadkill model with exclusive manual turn signal, guillotine-trunk hatch, and crucifixion gearshift knob. My brother had a stereo in the car that was worth more than the car itself. It was so loud that it could wake the dead, even four streets away. Don't even get me started on what that car said about *its* users. But with his twin Oldsmobile 98s, my dad was the king of Cincinnati, right? In production between 1940 and 1996, the Oldsmobile 98 was the brand's flagship model.

So what happened to the Oldsmobile brand? Known historically as General Motors' "executive innovator brand," Olds was hugely successful for decades. Oldsmobiles, designed to appeal to drivers who, according to GM, considered themselves "executive innovators" and "prosperous individualists," always featured the latest bells and whistles. When GM gave up on Oldsmobile and shut down the brand in 2004, the only people still driving them were my father's age. While other brands innovated around them and evolved their brands to tell powerful stories about new groups of drivers, Oldsmobile brand managers were asleep at the wheel, so to speak. There was a time in the '80s when General Motors tried to position the Oldsmobile to tech and engineering enthusiasts as a "Honda alternative." I wonder how that worked out for you, GM. If GM had taken a look around, they would have seen that there were still executive innovators and prosperous individualists out there. They just weren't driving Oldsmobiles. They were driving Audis and Acuras. So, if GM had managed the Oldsmobile brand properly, could it have adapted and stayed relevant? Absolutely. They could have made the story Oldsmobile told about its drivers relevant for generations to come.

Another example of a brand that went to the brand graveyard is Blackberry. The Blackberry may seem like a distant memory now, but just a few years ago (2009) it was the premier mobile gadget on the market. Remember when this device was so pervasive that people called it "CrackBerry?" Unable to embrace massive change in its industry, Blackberry lost its edge by being fearful of alienating its users if it changed too much too quickly. While consumers, enamored with full-color graphics, touch screens, and multimedia capabilities, were driving the smartphone revolution, Blackberry continued to focus on giving business users e-mail capabilities on the run. Blackberry failed to ascend to the top of the brand value pyramid and focused its energy on differentiating based upon functional benefits. Basically, Blackberry viewed its products as e-mail-enabled phones, while Apple marketed full-fledged mobile entertainment and communication hubs that made its users not only the arbiters of what's cool but also feel more in touch with not only their own worlds but the world at large.

## BRAND LONGEVITY

There are many examples of iconic brands that have been out there for a long time and yet have remained relevant with generations of new customers. It seems as if Coca-Cola has been around since the beginning of time, right? The Coca-Cola brand has endured because they have some of the best brand managers in the world. You and I have seen over our lifetime many, many iterations of Coca-Cola branding and marketing. However, the core story of Coca-Cola, as the Coca-Cola brand, remains the same. How Coke articulates its brand as something that transcends the products it produces and distributes—an optimistic, refreshing, happiness factory—has set them up to be relevant to an endlessly renewing group of consumers.

People are walking billboards for brands: from the shoes they wear, the coffee they drink, the cars they drive, to the books that they read; all those things convey who people are. Brands are part of your identity, whether you like it or not.

I've met people who say, "I'm not loyal to any particular brand. I'm not into brands. I don't like brands." That's part of their story, too. It's part of their personal brand that they're not buying into brands. "I'm brand agnostic. I'm just a price-driven purchaser." There's really no such thing as brand agnostic. Unless we're talking about a straight commodity, such as pork bellies, there is always a story about the product, and there's always a story that buying that product tells about the person using it.

## THE PSYCHOLOGY OF BRANDS

Psychologically, we all have a self concept—the person we want to see ourselves as, and the person we want to show to other people. Think of it as the outward-facing and the inward-facing versions of you. For many people, the two are the same. But for others, the outward and inward personas don't match. These people will often try to create another story for themselves, and they'll turn to brands to help them do it.

You probably know people who are proud vegans or vegetarians. That's a big part of their personal brand. For some "crunchy-granola" types, it's part of their brand. Same with the Paleo diet people and the CrossFit people. They identify with lifestyle "brands" because they tell a story about them. Have you ever noticed that gluten-free people proudly announce that they're gluten-free about 50 times a day and again at every meal? And then they are incensed when they go to a restaurant that doesn't have gluten-free options beyond the hamburger in a lettuce wrap? This is why. They like what it says about them. I'm apparently a terrible mother because I let my kid eat gluten.

## GLUTEN-FREE AS A BRAND

Here's a great example. Two years ago, I was running some focus groups for a grocery chain in the New York suburbs. We had a group of moms and primary grocery purchase influencers in these groups. In one particular group was a mom who was dressed to the nines in nonmatching animal print, a lot of sequins, and a lot of night makeup for the middle of the day. She had a very identifiable Long Island accent. She definitely was trying to tell a story about herself with everything she did, everything she said, and everything she was wearing.

When we began asking open-ended questions about food preferences, she said, "I'm not gluten intolerant, but I'm gluten-free," in her Long Island accent and then snapped her gum. She repeated it, "I'm not gluten intolerant, but I'm gluten-free. I buy all gluten-free products." I asked her why. She said, "I perceive that gluten-free products are just healthier, and that's how I show I care about what I put in my body." It's interesting that even the eating of gluten-free food is a part of the story this woman has created for herself. I guess she felt that buying gluten-free products made her a better mother, or maybe she was concerned about keeping up with the Joneses by eating gluten-free. Being gluten-free was such a part of this woman's brand that she proclaimed it to the group multiple times, and I thought it was amazing. Brands send a clear message about the user to both the outside world and to the customer him or herself.

## WHAT MAKES A BRAND SUCCESSFUL?

Here are the key ingredients for a successful brand. A brand has to connect with customers in a really strong way so that they purchase it and continue to repurchase it again and again. That loyalty comes from three things:

- First, customers must like the story that the brand tells about them.
- Second, the brand must offer one singular thing that customers won't get anywhere else, so it's indispensable to them.
- And third, the brand must help them to be the hero in their own stories.

In support of those elements, you need people to be aware of your brand (ideally be able to mention it off the top of their heads) and consider and purchase your brand in great volumes. Additionally, your brand needs to actually deliver on its promise. Keep in mind, though, there are many things that no amount of branding can fix. If your product sucks, it sucks. There are lots of examples out there of really awesome, very cool brands where the product did not deliver on the promise it made to buyers.

There's an ongoing joke in my family about this Rolex watch I bought years ago, and I still wear. Rolex is supposed to be this fine, Swiss-made timepiece brand that offers Swiss engineering and prestige. I bought the Rolex for the distinct reason that the Rolex brand exists: to show the world and myself that I had arrived. However, here's my dirty little secret: this thing keeps terrible time. At certain points, I clocked it at about a minute a day in lost time (pun intended). I've sent it in to Rolex in New York multiple times to have it fixed. They, in turn, sent it off to Geneva, and I was without it for weeks at a time. Nonplussed by my troubles, the fine watchmakers at Rolex intimated to me, "Sorry, lady. That's a feature." Nevertheless, I like the Rolex brand, and I like the story it tells about me. I just don't like that it can't tell time.

That's an example of how there can be a really strong brand, but if the product itself doesn't deliver on the promise, it becomes almost a joke. Rolex is a big joke among many watch enthusiasts. "Oh yeah, that Rolex looks beautiful, but it's a really crappy watch." You don't wear it to tell time, you wear it to tell a story. Luckily, we all have our smartphones to tell the precise time.

## WHAT MAKES A BRAND UNSUCCESSFUL?

There are two main reasons brands are unsuccessful. The

first is that the brand becomes associated with a negative message about its customers. The second is that the brand sends no message at all.

As I discussed in chapter one, "Brand or Be Branded," sending no message at all could spell doom for your brand. If you do not actively manage your brand, someone else will, and you probably won't like the end result.

I'm sad to say that I come across businesses all the time with no branding at all. It's quite common, actually. I'm a member of an organization called EO, which stands for Entrepreneurs' Organization. It's a sister organization to Young Presidents' Organization and World Presidents' Organization. EO is for entrepreneurs and for the founders and majority owners of private companies with revenues over one million dollars. It is very common among this group of people to see a business owner who has not worked on branding who suddenly experiences a plateau. The company gets to a certain level and growth stalls. The business owner is standing there scratching his head, saying, "Whoa, I can't grow over a certain amount. I feel like I've exhausted my market, and I don't know where the customers are."

Stalled growth and lost market share are common symptoms of a brand in crisis. In other words, these are companies that have lost their way when it comes to branding. By not really digging in and answering those three brand questions about themselves, they have not identified their core brand story. This is surprisingly prevalent.

Because I'm a lifelong student of branding, and I love everything about brands, it flummoxes me that somebody would start a company without going through the process of defining the underpinnings of their brand strategy. Why would so many very smart business owners do everything else right—sales, product, engineering, manufacturing, distribution—and then completely ignore one of the most essential elements of long-term growth? Yet it happens all the time. I believe it's because they simply do not understand the value and process of branding.

The other reason brands are unsuccessful is that they communicate a negative message about their customers. If customers like your product, but other people make fun of them for using it, or worse yet, customers are embarrassed or ashamed to use the brand, they'll stop being customers.

Stories from McDonald's and Olive Garden each illustrate this phenomenon.

Since 1955, McDonald's thrived on a brand that delivered an experience, not just hamburgers. The act of going to a McDonald's has always been more important than the food itself. At the core of the McDonald's brand is the promise of consistent, family-friendly fun offered at a good value. And the overall brand experience is designed to appeal to the child in your (adult) heart. However, with consumers paying increasing attention to the relationship among food, health, and chronic disease, McDonald's found itself in crisis. In about the early 2000s, the McDonald's brand started being credited with pushing unhealthy, artery-clogging cheap food for people who don't care what they put into their bodies. This negative brand association became a problem for customers, particularly powerful millennials who were starting to raise their own families. Exciting fast-casual restaurants with healthier menus that reflected more positively upon their patrons began to woo this customer group.

Being a smart company with a great brand strategy team, McDonald's came up with a fix. McDonald's launched a new healthy menu, featuring salads, wraps, and other low-fat, low-calorie options for health-conscious people. And they promoted the heck out of their new healthy menu. For a long time you couldn't drive down the highway without seeing a billboard with a delicious healthy salad nestled under those golden arches.

But here's the real story. The McDonald's healthy menu

items were a big bust in terms of sales, but a total success in terms of branding. Very few customers actually purchased those healthy meals and side options. Instead, customers continued to buy the chain's tasty, well-known Big Macs and fries. The ad blitz effectively evolved the public's perception of McDonald's from a chain that offered low-price unhealthy food, to one where you could get a salad and a heart-healthy turkey wrap with low-fat dressing. By heavily promoting the healthy menu items, the company turned around the problem of customers defecting from the brand because they didn't like the story the brand told about them. Even though customers weren't ordering the healthy food items, the mere *act* of McDonald's *offering* healthier items on its menu was enough for the brand to bond more strongly with customers.

I experienced a similar phenomenon during a project with Darden Restaurants, the parent company of Red Lobster and Olive Garden. Olive Garden was going through a McDonald's-like branding crisis. They did tons of research and found that, even though they wanted the brand to be known for family-friendly indulgence of customers' favorite Italian meal, many customers incorrectly and perhaps unfairly associated the brand with unhealthy meal choices.

Darden headquarters' response was to add a selection of healthier choices to their menus. However, similar to what happened at McDonald's, the Olive Garden's lighter and healthier dishes remained among their lowest-selling items. Even though the healthy menu items weren't big sellers, their mere presence on the menu was enough to begin the reinvigoration of the brand and draw in diners who could feel proud of what their choice said about them as individuals.

These are examples of brands trying to stop telling a negative story about their users and changing perception. McDonald's and Olive Garden will never be prime destinations for health-conscious eaters, and they know that. But they had to add healthy choices to their menus to address consumer backlash; people were saying, "If I go to McDonald's, I don't like what that says about me." People are still going to Olive Garden and ordering the unlimited bread sticks, but they don't mind nearly as much the story that the brand tells about them.

 **INTERVIEW**

WITH CHRIS TURNER, STAMPEDE CONSULTING, STAMPEDECONSULTING.COM

**Can you tell me about Stampede and the kind of work you do?**
Can you imagine how tough it must be for a member of the US Armed Forces to go from a job "fighting for America" to one where they might

be "fighting for Bank of America" once they leave the military? That's a rough transition that normally takes about 36 months to mentally shift over. Our company exists to provide service men and women with a soft landing in the form of cause-driven work and a team environment that looks and feels a lot like what they've become used to.

We recruit, train, and deploy veterans into political campaigns, knocking on doors, meeting voters, and building meaningful relationships. To use industry terms, we run grassroots field operations for pro-free-market candidates and causes—from the courthouse to the White House—in all 50 states. And we do it leveraging the talents of real-life American heroes. These soldiers fought for our freedoms. Our firm is trying to repay the favor in our own small way.

### Why is branding important in business and in politics?

Every single human being has a brand; it's not just corporate entities, or political candidates (who also happen to be humans, they just don't always act like it). If you don't understand the basic concept of branding, you'll never be able to understand how people see you or your company or product. We may see ourselves as complex organisms with diverse talents and virtues, but nobody else sees us that way.

Because your average American gets bombarded with something like 5,000 commercial messages a day, your brain is forced to boil things done to a single word or phrase as a descriptor. So that's all you get, the chance to own a single word or phrase in the minds of your prospects.

This is a blessing and a curse. A blessing in that it forces you to focus and a curse in that you have to dump a whole bunch of "new ideas" that you'd wanted to try.

**Brand or be branded. Is that true in politics?**
Deb is totally right on this. Politics is a perfect example.

A lot of people out there don't think they have to worry about this, but I will tell everyone in the world that they do. Many inexperienced first-time political candidates running for office think they can just put their names out there on yard signs or a billboard.

But if they don't tell people what their name *stands for*, I can guarantee you with 100 percent certainty that somebody is going to assign some negative meaning to that name in the minds of the voters. And it just might stick. Same is true outside of politics.

**What advice would you give to a company that really hasn't thought much about branding?**
My advice is, you're going nowhere. That's just the bottom line. You can have great product quality, great people, and great a process, but if you can't package it and merchandize it in a way that's compelling and stands out, it's not going anywhere.

There's a cacophony of marketing messages pounding customers every day. And the messages are coming from people who are just as resolute as you are about the benefits of their products.

We always say in the political world that if you believe that your cause is just—and in the private sector world it would be if you believe that your product is really going to make a positive difference in people's lives—then you have a moral obligation to learn how to win the game. Understanding branding is part of that.

If your product isn't branded in a way that "makes sense" to the customer, it won't sell. If it doesn't sell, don't blame the customer for just not "getting it." Blame yourself.

**Is politics just sort of a super-intense form of personal branding?**
It's intense in the sense that it's scrutinized a lot more than your average product brand, that's for sure. I think people are frustrated with politics because they don't know what the political brands stand for anymore. I mean that from a pure branding and marketing sense. They don't know what they're buying anymore, and I think that's one reason why people's frustration levels are up.

The same is true for companies and their products. When a company starts off with a really great product and they offer X, and then they move into something totally different, it confuses customers. If you start off selling the best face cream ever and then a few weeks later your M&A team gets the idea to buy a screwdriver factory and you want to get into that business, don't be surprised when the customers are confused by what you're offering them. And customer confusion is the scariest thing in business. Because confused customers, like confused voters, don't buy.

# FOUR

# WHAT IS THE ONE THING?

**"**

*I think it's really important to tell your story early, even before you launch. Especially with something that's competitive in nature. It's almost like a company mission; your brand is your mission, in my opinion.*
HEATHER ZIDELL, CFO (CHIEF FROSTING OFFICER), TRAILERCAKES

I always ask my clients, "What is the singular thing that customers get from you that they can't get anywhere else?" The client usually answers, "Our product is faster, better, smaller, bigger, taller, cheaper, longer, more flexible, redder, pinker, or sexier than anything else." Wrong answer! That's a list of functional benefits delivered by your product's features. Your uniqueness is *not* one of your product features.

This chapter focuses on that one thing—your brand story's uniqueness and how that uniqueness, unlike product features, can create irrational loyalty. Why are stories so special compared to product features? Stories point to a singular thing that the customers can't get anywhere else.

The story of your brand should convey a singular idea or concept that your brand can own. It may be a certain *combination* of product features, benefits, and attributes. But it also likely includes the way you deliver an experience and the relationship you have with your customers. Singularity narrows your focus and bonds you more strongly to your customers because they truly understand what your brand is about. This chapter is about figuring out the one thing you provide that no one else can.

## VOLVO'S ONE THING

Let's take the example of Volvo automobiles. With regard to singularity, Volvo is about safety. There is just this automatic association of Volvo cars with notions of safety. That is truly a concept that's ownable by Volvo. That's not to say that there aren't other brands out there that are safe. Of course there are. But Volvo owns the *concept* of safety when you think about automobiles. Why do consumers believe Volvos are so safe? A combination of features such as the first inflatable side curtain airbags and rollover protection systems, as well as technology, reputation, history, and branding.

The functional and emotional benefits provided by your company's features are in the middle of the pyramid, but the *combination* of those features with your self-expressive benefits creates the singular, ownable concept that is associated with your brand. Volvo owners usually have children, and they like being safe on the road. But what they really like is sending a message to the world that says something like, "My choice to drive my children to school in this Volvo shows that I care more about my family than you." Sure, there are other automobile brands out there that are safe. But only one of them can be the "safety" brand. The choice to drive the safety brand of cars tells an even more dialed-in story about the driver than simply driving a safe Toyota or Honda.

Singularity is important. Being singular means having something that's ownable and unique to you and being consistent about delivering that throughout your entire business. That's part of writing your brand story. Volvo does a really good job of this. Everything they say is about reinforcing this singular idea of safety. Everything they do is about delivering on the promise of safety. Their values and beliefs as a brand are that people deserve protection when they go out there into the dangerous world. That comes across consistently throughout their entire brand experience.

So how did Volvo come to own that one thing? It's the combination of design, engineering, safer equipment, manufacturing processes, their relationship with customers, their distribution and sales network, the way they sell, and the way they train their sales associates in the dealerships; all that stuff reinforces the brand and leads to the singularity of safety.

## FINDING YOUR ONE THING

Putting all those things together and articulating the totality of the brand is where you come up with your singularity. Your brand's singularity is the essence of the brand that no other brand can own. I went to a party last Friday night and this guy told me, "You are not like anybody else I have ever met in my life. You are a singular human being. You are completely unique."

## BRANDER BEWARE

### *The Danger of Not Being Singular*

Clients often ask me about the dangers of not being singular. Remember Xerox? At one time Xerox was so singular a brand that their very name became synonymous with the promise they actually delivered. There was a time when a photocopy was actually called a "Xerox." While they were enjoying their success as the copier company in the '70s and '80s, they flirted with the idea of expanding their brand into business and personal computers. However, the idea never took off and cost Xerox millions of dollars. To consumers and business-purchase influencers alike, Xerox was copiers. They were not computers or monitors or disk drives. As a result of losing focus from their singular, ownable position as a copier brand, Xerox made their brand more complicated and created opportunities for other competitors to gain ground against them. Singularity brings you focus. A narrow, unchanging focus is more important to a brand's strength than the mass appeal of a product. Without a narrow focus, your brand lacks relevance and a core idea. Without consistency, your brand will never have a firm root in your customers' hearts and minds.

I asked him, "Where does that come from? What about me is not like anyone else?"

He said, "It's not any one thing. It's all of these things put together."

It's sort of like the French concept of "*je nais se quois*," which translates in English to, "I don't know what." However, in the case of branding, you not only need to know what it is, but your customers must be able to experience that feeling or promise from your brand. *That* is what I mean by singularity.

The next question you need to answer for your brand is, what are all of the things that, when you put them together, make you truly you? It's not just that one feature your brand has that nobody else has. It's that, *plus* a bunch of other stuff. It's the everything-ness of your brand. It's what makes your brand a unique snowflake unlike everybody else.

Being singular makes you indispensable to your customers. What exactly do I mean by indispensable? This means, if I took the product away from you or made you live without this brand, you would feel some sort of loss. Or, more realistically, if your local grocery store stopped carrying the product, you'd drive across town to a store that does. That's what I mean by indispensability, and that's one of the foundations of irrational loyalty. As we discussed briefly in chapter one, a good example that I think defines irrational loyalty is Apple. The iPhone, in particular, is the greatest example of this.

## SINGULARITY, INDISPENSABILITY, AND IRRATIONAL LOYALTY

Samsung and Apple phones are so similar looking that if I see somebody using one of these two smartphones, I have to look really, really closely to see what kind it is. Physically, they are virtually indistinguishable from each other. However, the story that Apple tells about its user varies vastly from the story that Samsung tells about its user.

Samsung's product is technologically superior. The company's phones have more processing memory. They have more storage space. They have better glass. They have better touch-screen functionality. They are thinner. They are faster and higher performing. They often cost less. But Apple succeeds based on how strongly the brand has bonded with its users through representing a singular idea while telling a story about its users.

What makes the Apple brand indispensable is the idea that Apple is about a concept. The Apple brand is about design, form, and function all elegantly working together. It's about looking cool to others and having a positive and open outlook on life. It's about being creative, connected, and thriving in a digital world. Apple's singular idea is magic. It almost doesn't matter what Apple product we're talking about; they all deliver on the singular promise of magic for its users (Remember the launch of the iPod? "1,000 songs in your pocket.") The Samsung smartphone brand is above all about performance—delivered through product leadership and engineering. Apple is a concept brand; Samsung is a product brand. So while these two companies produce similar-looking products, the singular ideas that make these brands indispensable to their respective users are vastly different.

If you look closely at the people who use the Samsung phone and the people who use the iPhone, there's a difference between them. There was a study done a few years ago by the website Hunch.com. Researchers compared Android phone users to iPhone users and concluded that there are significant psychographic and behavioral differences between them. The study found that people who use the iPhone tend to be more positive, more outwardly focused, more extroverted, and more optimistic, as well as happier, whereas Android users were a bit more serious, reserved, analytical, introverted, and introspective. This is a good example of how brand choices really are a part of an individual's self concept and often accurately reflect the self-image they want to project.

# ANDROID VERSUS APPLE iOS:

## Psychographic Differences

According to research conducted by the website Hunch.com, differences between Android and iOS users abound. Here are a few interesting data points from the study.

- The study showed that iOS users are 37 percent more likely to have a graduate degree than Android users.
- Android users are 86 percent more likely to live in the country than iOS users.
- The results showed that iOS users are 50 percent more likely than Android users to have traveled to more than five countries.
- Android users are 24 percent more likely to have a song for a ringtone than iOS users.
- Android users are more likely to shop for clothing at Brooks Brothers and Ralph Lauren, whereas iOS users are more likely to shop at Tom Ford and Marc Jacobs.
- Apple iOS users are more likely to watch HBO, Bravo, and BBC. Android users are more likely to watch Discovery Channel, Comedy Central, and ESPN.

Who knew your choice of a phone said so much about you?

You can find the blog post and infographic here: http://www.bandwidthblog.com/2011/08/16/personality-characteristics-of-iphone-vs-android-users-infographic/

When Samsung launches a new phone or a new tablet, you don't see people camping out on sidewalks overnight with tents and lawn chairs and ordering pizza in front of the store to be the first ones to buy it when the doors open. But that does happen at the launch of every new iPhone model (the Android crowd calls those people "iSheep"). That's irrational loyalty. Every one of those people knows they can just walk into the store a week later without waiting in line and buy the same phone for the same price. And I guarantee those people already have the previous version of the iPhone in their hands. But it doesn't matter. They want it now. That is the pinnacle of irrational loyalty.

## CAN THAT TYPE OF SUCCESS BE DUPLICATED?

Yes, that kind of success can be duplicated. We see it all over the place. I see it in my own life. For many years, I drove Volvos. Even though the cars were boxy and ugly and my Volvo SUV drove like a freaking Mack truck, I was loyal to the Volvo brand. I had a young child. I felt if I bought a Mercedes-Benz that somehow I would be cheating on Volvo.

Eventually I no longer liked the story Volvo told about me as a person. I started to feel a little bit boxed in to the "I'm a better parent than you because I drive *the* safe car" brand story. So I had to seek out another brand. And then I became irrationally loyal to another brand to the point that I was, like, "Oh, it's time for a new car. I better go get another one of these." I was irrationally loyal to that brand for nine years and then all of a sudden I woke up one day and I'm like, "Oh my gosh, I am not my grandmother. Why am I driving this car?"

There are actually several brands in my life that I feel like I would be cheating on if I bought one of their competitors. For instance, take the toothpaste I use. I am so fiercely loyal to this brand that even if the competing brand is on sale for a fraction of the price of my favorite, I won't buy it. Even though the brands are virtually indistinguishable from each other and have all the same ingredients and features, in my mind I'm a Colgate person, not a Crest person. I just won't cheat.

## WHEN IS BRANDING NOT IMPORTANT?

Is there any business, product, or category where branding is not important? Actually, yes. In the world of commodities, branding is not important. This includes any homogeneous product sold by the freight train-full, such as bulk corn, rice, oats, soybeans, sugar, steel, and coal. By the very definition of commodities, there's no brand. But that's really the only business where branding is unimportant. So, unless you're selling pork bellies, your company needs a brand strategy.

## HOW EARLY TO BRAND?

Even if nobody has heard of your company before, it's essential to begin the branding process as soon as possible. One of the things I do in my practice is coaching and mentoring startups in accelerators, at small business incubators, and at investor pitch competitions. In addition to the core brand-strategy firm, I run another business called InvestorPitches.com. We work with early-stage companies to help them tell their stories effectively to an investor audience in order to secure funding.

I always say, "Brand early, often, and always." It's never too early to start branding. For an unfunded startup, it may be too early to invest significantly in ad spend and building a visual brand. But it's never too early to understand your brand strategy from your customers' point of view. At the very least, I encourage startups in their very early phase, while they're going through the process of figuring out if there's a product-market fit, to understand the answers to the three questions we first introduced in this book's introduction.

As a startup, if you do nothing else, answer those three questions. This process gives you your brand's North Star. Your North Star gives you direction and points you toward where you're going. The best thing about branding at the early stage is it helps you identify not only what you're going to do but also, and more importantly, what you're *not* going to do. It's really easy as a startup, or an early-stage company, to be opportunistic and float around to wherever the money is and to try to be all things to all customers instead of focusing. But that doesn't work long term, and you can't build a lasting brand on that strategy.

You can make more strategic, thoughtful, and deliberate decisions about your business when you know direction-ally where you're going. The customer is always at the center of that. I'm old enough that I've been through a couple of comings of the technology industry and the Internet. I actually worked in the technology industry for the first half of my career, so I've seen it firsthand. Traditionally, the technology industry has been about building better mousetraps. Now it's less about mice and more about special sauce.

## WHAT IS YOUR SPECIAL SAUCE?

As a brand, if you think of your own story as the story of your customer, you will always win. Then, even if your competitors start offering consumers more advanced fea-tures with their products, people will care less about those new features and more about the sum total of everything you offer because of what the brand says about them and the singular concept you represent.

Singularity, knowing and communicating your one thing, is really hard, though. It's ideal if you can boil your one thing down to one word or one concept. But this is really hard for brands to do and it takes a lot of time. It's not as simple as driving a stake in the ground and declaring, "This is what we stand for." No. It's something earned through being able to deliver a complete brand experience, something that's comprehensive.

Think of your one thing as your special sauce. Did you ever see the Julia Roberts movie *Mystic Pizza*? (I guess I'm dating myself here. But stay with me.) The pizzas were unique and delicious and out of this world because of their special sauce. The special sauce has many ingredients, all of which are available to your competitors as well. But it's the unique way you combine those ingredients and cook them and throw in some kitchen magic that makes the sauce special. Competitors can't duplicate that.

One of the famous case studies taught in MBA programs around the country is the Tylenol poisoning murders. Someone deliberately poisoned bottles of Tylenol with cyanide and people died. In response, Johnson & Johnson pulled millions of bottles of Tylenol off store shelves. No one in the entire country was buying Tylenol. But guess what? Johnson & Johnson was able to recover because their brand was about trust and transparency and openness and dealing with problems head on. So even though Tylenol killed people, the brand recovered, and it is now stronger than it's ever been.

To this day, I will buy Tylenol over cheaper generic acetaminophen because the Tylenol brand to me means I can trust it. Even though the generic product is exactly the same formulation, and it has the same features and the same benefits, I still pay more for Tylenol. Because what does buying brand name Tylenol say about me? It says that I value the health and safety of my family and myself above all.

## START WITH WHY

A lot of the branding strategy we do at Sol Marketing comes from my strong belief that you have to start with identifying your "why." Why are you making and selling this product? Identify why you're passionate about it and be mission and passion-driven about what you're doing. The best results always come from creating brands around what you're singularly compelled to do.

In the first tech boom in the 1990s, Silicon Valley was a bunch of solutions in search of problems. There was no *why* for many of the startups. Smart and strategic engineers with technology-driven mousetraps typified the early

> ## WORTH WATCHING
>
> If you want to learn more about the concept of "why,"
> please check out Simon Sinek's powerful TED Talk on
> YouTube titled "Start with Why."

days of the tech industry. But the industry has evolved to identifying, first of all, whether mice are a problem and then investigating the impact of that mouse problem. New philosophies in technology innovation now also ask the question, if having mice is a problem, is this a problem that needs solving? And can we solve it with technology?

Now, in order to compete, startups have to be in a position to demonstrate three things. First, that there really is a problem. Second, that they have a unique solution to the problem. And third, that they have a vision for why they want to solve that problem and what the world is going to look like after they do. In other words, they must have a very clear reason *why* they exist.

For example, dozens of companies are marketing small business customer relationship management (CRM) apps right now. The competition is fierce. In order for your startup to receive funding with a $250,000 seed round and then actually go to market and get some paying customers and scale, you have to be able to *tell the story of your brand*. So, long before you can close a series A, or even a seed round, you need to work hard to answer why you exist for your customers.

In the small business CRM example, startup founders should never go into an investor pitch meeting and focus just on product features or a product demo alone. As we've discussed, product features, and even some of the functional and emotional benefits they provide, are not entirely unique and are open for imitation by competitors. Perhaps even better than startup founders, savvy investors know this. Think back to the brand values pyramid—product features are the stuff at the bottom of the pyramid. That's the ante just to get into the game. You sell investors on your *why* and on your brand *story*. Focus on *why* you're doing what you do.

 **INTERVIEW**

Heather Zidell is the cofounder and chief frosting officer at a cool startup bakery in Dallas called Trailercakes. Heather is a natural-born branding genius, and she has learned a ton about launching a startup brand in a crowded space.

**What was your background before you got into frosting?**
I spent over 22 years in digital advertising and sales. So being the CFO is a big change for me.

**Why was it important to create and maintain your company's brand early on?**
You want to be different from everybody else. At least in the cupcake world, everybody has a competitor, and when we founded Trailercakes, it was going to be different. I don't want to say there's a cupcake store on every block, but there are cupcakes all over the place. We really wanted to set our brand apart from the get-go as something very different, and find a unique way to do it.

**Can't you just worry about that a few years down the road? Why do you need to do it sooner rather than later?**
You want people to experience your brand, especially in a small busi-

ness when you're starting out. I think it's critical to have an experience with all of your customers. Especially with what we've created, we wanted a lot of word-of-mouth marketing. Even at the very beginning, we really wanted people to understand what we were doing. And that's why I think it's really important to tell your story early, even before you launch. Especially with something that's competitive in nature. It's almost like a company mission; your brand is your mission, in my opinion.

**How have you done this in your business?**
Through our marketing, through our website, and through our trailer, which is like a life-size logo for our company. Our cupcake brand is about nostalgia. We want you to come in and not only experience a delicious cupcake, but we want it to remind you of your childhood. Our focus is "Happiness in the Frosting." Everything on the top of our cupcakes has to do with something from the nostalgic period of when I grew up, the '70s and '80s.

**You say that your branding is in everything, from your sonic identity to what the cupcakes look like. Can you explain?**
We're about the '70s and '80s. Some cupcakes have a Nutter Butter on the top or a Pop-Tart. When you come in and buy a cupcake, you're going to see a Pop-Tart and go, "Wow, this reminds me of the seventies or eighties." But also you're going to hear nostalgic music. Whenever we take our trailer out to events, or if you come into our store, nothing will be on the speakers except '70s and '80s music. We have people who actually dance to our music when they come in the store. It's

not just about promoting products; in fact, it has very little to do with promoting products. It's more about engaging with your customers. I think social media is a great place to experience a brand, have people engage with the brand and what it's trying to do. Everybody knows who Fonzie is. We'll have contests where if you walk in and do your best "Ayyy" you'll walk out with a dozen cupcakes.

**The trailer is a part of your brand as well?**
Yes. The trailer, from a branding perspective, I think it has really succeeded. Our trailer's name is Bubbles. The trailer has an identity. Our followers on Facebook, Instagram, and Twitter love Bubbles. Our customers don't say, "Where's your trailer?" They write, "Where's Bubbles?" People really like it. "Where's Bubbles?" That's a key part of our brand that I think sets us apart from competitors and other businesses. There are pictures of Bubbles on our Facebook page.

**What advice would you give to business owners who have not really thought much about branding?**
They need to think about it, and they need to think about, "What do you want your customers to believe when they think about your business?" The more authentic you can be in telling your story, the easier it is to execute a plan to grow the brand.

# FIVE

# WHO IS THE HERO?

**"**

*We got the branding done a year and a half before we even launched the product. So brand was the first obstacle I took on. I knew that I could get further and have more doors opened as long as branding was the first thing we accomplished.*

CARY PREWITT, CHIEF GUNSLINGER, GUNS & OIL BEER COMPANY

We've talked about the importance of your brand's story. But just like in the movies, every good story has a hero. So in the story your brand tells about its customers, who is the hero? This chapter explains why a brand should strive to make the customer the hero in his or her own story. This is true whether the customer is an individual consumer or an executive working within an organization. Everyone wants to be the protagonist in his or her own story.

I want to explain this concept a little further, and then give some examples of those heroics. Being the hero, in the context of a brand story, doesn't mean that you have to go out and do epic things such as parachuting behind enemy lines, saving the world, or slaying dragons. We're talking about everyday heroism.

Heroism can be something as simple as making a dinner that everyone loves, or getting the kids to eat veggies and then brush their teeth and go to bed on time. Everyday heroism is what makes you feel competent, empowered, happy, effective, accomplished, and successful. In short, it makes you feel like a hero. And when you feel empowered and accomplished, that puts you in the mood for sex. Branding is sex because when your successful brand story makes the customer feel like the hero in her own story, she wants to get laid.

Here is a very simplistic example of a hero story. Have you ever had that feeling right from the moment you got out of bed that it is going to be a great day? You go and do your morning workout, and you set a personal record for the number of reps you do on a particular machine at a particular weight. Today is the day you shaved 30 seconds off your pace on your treadmill run. You think to yourself, "I am on top of the world." Then you leave the gym and get into your car, and on your way to work, you make every traffic light.

## FEELING LIKE THE HERO

This is something that never happens in real life, but just go with me for a minute. You pull into the parking lot at work and you find rock star parking right in front of the building. Yes! You walk into the office and there is already a hot pot of coffee brewing, and someone brought your favorite kind of bagels. People are bustling about the office. You sit down. Your 9:00 a.m. meeting suddenly cancels, so you have 30 minutes to yourself to catch up on those 8,000 unread e-mails in your inbox (In my case, it's closer to 10,000.). This run of good luck continues throughout the day. You completely eliminate every possible thing that could potentially be a day ruiner.

By the time five o'clock rolls around, instead of being a typical day where you experienced a soul-crushing workload, you leave the building feeling energized and confident, as if you have the world on a string. On the drive home, you make every traffic light, and when you arrive home, your loved one is there. He or she has cooked an amazing meal, and you sit down to enjoy it. The kids are all quiet and well behaved—no fighting, no complaining, none of the regular bedtime delays. When eight or nine o'clock comes and you and your loved one are together, how do you feel? You feel euphoric. You feel relaxed. You feel sexy. You feel like a hero. You feel like you want to do it. This is the chapter of the book where we talk about how branding is about sex.

## BRANDING IS SEX

What happens when you feel like you have the world on a string and everything is going your way, and the story of your life is progressing in a positive direction? You feel good. You feel *randy*. You feel like you want to grab your partner—or a stranger—and you want to do it. All branding is about getting people laid. It really is. It's not just about being sexy. It's about having sex. When the story you tell yourself truly makes you feel heroic, you feel your power, and you're in the mood for having sex.

When I say "having sex" and "getting laid," it could literally mean getting naked and grabbing your ankles. But it may also have a figurative meaning of being praised, complimented, and fawned over, as well as getting your ego stroked and being shown appreciation by your partner or children. Which sometimes feels even better than sex (at least in my experience— don't quote me on that).

## HOW DOES YOUR BRAND GET THE CUSTOMER LAID?

When I consult with clients and they struggle with who the hero is and the story their brand tells about them, the shortcut is to ask, "How does your product or service get the customer laid?" I literally ask my clients this very question. And it works. That is the question you must ask yourself in this chapter. How does this brand get a person laid?

Allrecipes is a brand that helps customers feel like a hero in the kitchen. Having the world on a string and feeling empowered and enjoying a wonderful home-cooked meal where everything is easy makes you want to take a roll in the hay with your partner. That is the essence of the Allrecipes hero story: How does the customer prepare a delicious dinner that will please her children and her spouse and make her feel triumphant in the kitchen? The hero story for customers cooking dinner is solving the problem of what's for dinner tonight and making sure they have a frictionless experience in the kitchen and at the dinner table that leaves everybody happy and satisfied. It's a feeling that is so good that they want to jump in bed with their significant other.

This narrative applies to business to business brands as well. That dude in procurement who makes the decision about which enterprise resource planning software he purchases for the manufacturing arm of his company also has a story in which he is the hero. His decision to buy that software is part of that story. Your goal as a brand marketer is to understand the stories your customers are trying to tell and make those customers into the heroes in those stories.

The most successful and profitable brands in the world are created around people. There is an emotional connection that can happen for the purchasing manager who's buying microprocessors in the same way there is an emotional connection that exists between my shoes and me. Let me give an example of this.

## THE IT MANAGER AS HERO

My company works extensively with Dell Inc. on the enterprise side of their business, the part of their company that sells systems and solutions to the IT managers of other businesses. Traditionally, Dell treated enterprise

IT managers as if they were robots—completely devoid of feelings and abstract thoughts. What we know here at Sol Marketing is that each of those IT managers has a story that they are writing for their own lives. That story involves them, eventually, getting laid. And if your brand can help that happen, you'll have a loyal customer.

When I am working with Dell or with any other company that sells technology products and services to IT purchase influencers, I want the company to step outside of itself as a brand and step into the hearts and minds of its IT manager customer. That IT manager is a human being who has wants and needs and desires. Conjure up an image of that person in your mind. Ask yourself, "What does success look like for that person? What does getting laid look like for him or her?" Then ask yourself, "How does my product/brand/service do that for them?"

Dell sells a lot of servers. The servers Dell sells go into racks that live in computer rooms and data centers all over the world. Servers don't feel cool when you hold them in your hand. To the unindoctrinated, run-of-the-mill human, a server probably looks like a mess of metal and plastic and wires. On the surface, a server just isn't that sexy, nor is the Dell brand. A server is not like a bottle of perfume, a designer leather jacket, or a Ferrari. IT managers are Dell's main customers for servers.

So let's do an exercise for illustration's sake. For purposes of this exercise, take a walk in an IT manager customer's shoes. Let's say this particular customer is a 47-year-old man. He works at a nationwide furniture retailer with stores in 22 states. He has a need to put together an IT program in which all of the remote stores can send their transaction and inventory data to a central location at night. That requires a lot of computing power, remote access capabilities, and powerful servers and software—none of which are very sexy. All of those things must work together flawlessly.

If you think about what is *un*sexy about this IT manager's job, it is a phone call from a store manager in the middle of the night. Also unsexy is when the chief information officer comes down on him hard and says, "We did not pull data last night, and we don't have the store-by-store results. My boss is up my ass for sales results, and because of an IT infrastructure issue and a network failure, we cannot do that." These are terribly unsexy things that can happen to this guy, and they absolutely can prevent him from getting laid.

The essence of brand strategy is to take that unsexiness and turn it around. To do that, you should ask, "How do we actually get that guy laid?" Dell does that by offering reliable products that they stand behind and develop with

IT purchase influencers' needs in mind. Dell's enterprise brand is most concerned with making sure the IT manager has the best experience he possibly can have working with their product. Dell is trying to give that IT manager the world-on-a-string feeling we described earlier in this chapter by delivering on its promises to him.

Dell's goal is to make that IT manager the hero in his own story. It's right there in their current brand manifesto: "The Power to Do More." Dell gives an IT manager the power to do more, not only with IT but also in his life overall. Dell gets him home for dinner on time and inspires him with the confidence that everything back at work is functioning flawlessly, even when he's not there. Dell's industry-leading uptime and reliability get him laid by preventing phone calls in the middle of the night when stores cannot send their data to the home office. Dell makes sure the boss is not standing in the IT manager's office at 8:00 a.m. the next morning growling, "Where have you been? The network crashed." These are the things Dell does to help him become the hero in the story of his life. Sure, Dell products are reliable, scalable, flexible, durable, innovative, and a good value. But it's the way they make, sell, deliver, and support those products that enable their customers to "do more."

## BRANDING IS NOT A STEP-BY-STEP PROCESS

Remember I said early in this book that the answer to the question of "When to brand?" is early, often, and always. When you answer the three big questions in chapters three, four, and five, you will take steps toward nailing down your brand strategy. But I wouldn't call this a step-by-step process. It's not as if you just answer those three questions once and you're done. Answering those questions is actually an ongoing exercise that should happen throughout the life of the brand. Branding is not something that takes place at a single point in time.

Similarly, documenting and living your brand values pyramid is an ongoing process. Remember, you are in a competitive environment with changing customer needs and market forces that are beyond your control. For instance, new products come along and offer the same benefits as yours, but in a different way. Or a startup launches a revolutionary product that's a complete category killer—like Uber did to taxicabs. You could end up competing in ways you never imagined, and all of a sudden, you have to reinvent your brand and your story. So the branding conversation is something that needs to take place all the time. You have to be in constant touch with your customers and your customers' needs, or subject yourself to the risk of becoming irrelevant.

How does a brand remain relevant to customers? A brand can stay relevant by always answering those three big questions.

- What does your brand say about your customers?
- What is the singular thing your brand delivers that customers can't get from anyone else?
- How do you make your customer a hero in the story of his or her own life?

I recommend that you continually answer those questions just to find out if anything has changed. And if something has changed, figure out how it has changed.

These are the underpinnings of brand strategy. And every time you go to market with a new product or even a new marketing campaign, you need to revisit the three questions.

## WHO DOES THE BRANDING AT A COMPANY?

Who should be responsible for the brand strategy at your company? It doesn't matter if you are a small business owner with five employees, or you're the CEO of a billion-dollar company, the answer is the same. Branding is *everybody's* responsibility.

Organizations that benefit the most from branding are the ones where every single person inside the company is a steward of their brand. The companies that do the best are the ones in which the people at the top of the organization lead the charge for branding. In those companies, it's often the CEO, but it's also the COO and the CFO and the CTO and basically anybody with a "C" in their title who takes up the cause and drives the strategy through the entire organization. In order for branding to work, every single person must feel ownership and responsibility for the brand. And the leadership must drive that into every nook and cranny of the organization so that people are walking the brand talk. It has to start from the top.

Contrary to commonly held beliefs, branding is not the responsibility of some random marketing manager or the person in charge of campaigns or the person with "brand" in his or her title. Branding is the responsibility of every single person in the business. Once you have answered the three questions for your business and you understand what's in the top of your brand values pyramid, then every single thing every single person in the company does should align with delivering on that promise. Some people call this walking the talk, or drinking the Kool-Aid, or eating your own dog food. Whatever you want to call it, it's important that it starts from the top and permeates throughout the entire organization.

Cary Prewitt is the CEO and founder of a beer brand called Guns & Oil. It's a Texas beer brand. He set out from the beginning not to be a brew master, but to build a lifestyle brand. He's an entrepreneurial wunderkind. Does the world need another beer brand? No. But he ventured out there to create a brand from the ground up. He started by focusing on the brand first, product second.

**How did you first decide to launch a beer brand?**

I've always been an entrepreneur. I started my first company at 21 that did tickets and travel packages to major sporting events. It was very high-end and luxury focused. It was a good time, but it wasn't something I was happy with long term. The margins were shrinking, and it was not a great business. So I was sort of looking for a longer-term project that would be a lot of fun and that we could turn into a lifestyle brand and a values-driven brand.

While drinking one night, I came up with Guns & Oil. Knowing it was going to take some money to create the beer, I actually got my branding done first. I met with about 15 branding agencies and found one that really seemed to get it. You could see the lightbulb turn on. They saw my brand as John Wayne and the Wild West. It clicked.

**So you created the branding first and the product second?**

We got the branding done a year and a half before we even launched the product. So brand was the first obstacle I took on. I knew that I could get further and have more doors opened as long as branding was the first thing we accomplished. So it was really an important step. It allowed me to get meetings I could otherwise not have gotten because of the fact that our branding was clean, it looked really good, and people just took it seriously. It just helped us get a lot further a lot quicker.

So we branded first, then I went and found a brewer, and then I went and found an operator. So I really built this company backward. For us it was the right way to go. And it helped us get to where we are today. People absolutely love our brand, and it pulls very well off the grocery store shelves because it's clean, it's pretty, and it represents people.

**So how did you create the brand?**

Before you launch a brand, you first have to figure out if you have customers for your brand. You can spend a lot of money on research, but we didn't. With ours it sort of clicked right away. People were drawn to it. I do believe you have to be willing to put in the time money and energy to do the research. And if people aren't drawn to your brand and it's a consumer product, you need to take a step back and say, "Is this a branding issue, or is this a values issue?" In other words, is it that people don't like the way my brand looks, or they don't like what it stands for and don't believe it represents them? I believe that's a very important distinction to make.

**What are the brand values of Guns & Oil?**

Our values are the great American values: boldness, character, opportunity, grit, and innovation. These are the things that made America great. They represent the American dream and the swagger behind our country. It's pretty easy to get excited about those. And I believe a beer is a badge. When you hold it in your hand, people want to hold something that represents them, or represents a feeling they have. So there are values behind it. Making sure your brand can stick from a values standpoint is absolutely the most important thing. And making sure your customers believe in your mission, vision, and values.

**How did you do customer research?**

We didn't have a huge budget for customer research. I just started putting our logo and designs on Facebook and sharing them with friends to see what people thought. The feedback we got was always overwhelmingly positive. A few negative responses, but vastly positive. Then we threw a big beer tasting party, and we had 150 people show up to taste test and vote on our first beer.

We invited 200, and 150 showed up. We were thrilled. People knew we were onto something. It was mostly for research, but we also invited people who could get us to the next level. And it worked. We invited our network of friends and others.

**How much did that cost?**

Research doesn't always have to cost money. We had a great venue and it only cost us $1,000 to rent. The beer cost was very cheap.

You don't have to do things the expensive way. Every time we've done things the expensive way we usually ended up throwing money down the drain. In most cases, there are ways to do research much more efficiently and for way less cost. Be resourceful. We tried radio advertising, but we stopped it. It was too expensive, and it's hard to make people feel when they hear your brand on the air three times in an hour.

We threw another event and invited 80 bartenders to show up. They got to help choose our second flavor of beer with their votes. They loved it. Just be sure you make decisions and throw events that provide maximum bang for the buck. It's not about throwing events for the sake of socializing.

We also spent a lot of time interacting with customers. We also sell merchandise on our website, so that's a sign that people like the branding too.

# *SIX*

# THIS IS NOT A SHOE

**SO NOW THAT YOU'VE ANSWERED THE THREE BIG QUESTIONS,** how do you start putting what you've learned about your customers into practice? Remember, the point of this kind of brand strategy process is to put the customer at the center of the brand. Your brand is about the customer; the brand is not about you. That requires you to think carefully about who your customer is. The first thing that I recommend doing is identifying and profiling your *ideal* customer.

## THE TRADITIONAL MARKETING METHOD: SEGMENTATION

The strategy of building your brand for an ideal customer is the reverse of the traditional marketing method you leaned in business school. Traditional marketing has always taught us to think about *segmenting* and *dividing* markets. When you're bringing a new product to market, the traditional textbook methodology is to think about who are *all* the potential people who could possibly buy this product. And then what are all the potential use cases, what are the possible purchase channels, and what are their reasons for buying and not buying the product?

Traditional marketing methods tell us to identify as many potential audiences as we can and then divide them further based upon demographics, or shopping behaviors, or desires and attitudes. That's segment marketing, or segmentation. Segmentation is the practice of creating groups within groups. When we talk about marketing segments, we are describing groups in which the people are maximally similar to one another, but then the groups themselves are maximally dissimilar. When you go through this type of segmentation, you might say, "Okay, we have four target segments. We've got the busy mom segment, we've got the single guy segment, we've got the people who are looking for an easy solution segment, and the empty nesters."

Using that old way of thinking often means taking your brand message and dividing it rather than multiplying it. Segment marketing suggests that you're going to create a different brand experience for each of those different audiences. When you start dividing and segmenting your market, you start creating more and more marketing messages that are dissimilar from each other. If not managed, that practice can dilute your brand's impact.

I'm not against segment marketing. In fact, part of my company does quantitative psychographic research with the goal of creating and identifying market segments and then coming up with marketing strategies and tactics for companies to go after those segments. Segments are for designing and marketing products and services to particular groups. But when you create your brand, you need to look to what's similar among all of those segments to create a singular brand that is "for" a singular customer *archetype*. That customer archetype is called the "ideal customer," and it's an in-depth profile of the customer who is *most* highly predictive of a brand's success.

## IDENTIFYING YOUR IDEAL CUSTOMER

Identifying the ideal customer archetype is not the same as segment marketing, and this task shouldn't replace your segmentation activities. The ideal customer archetype is something that serves as a guiding principle for everything you do in branding and gives you a singular, highly identifiable customer persona toward which to point your brand's story. The ideal customer archetype is a fleshed out, detailed, hypothetical profile of your absolute *ideal* customer. Intimately knowing this profile will help keep you anchored while you create brand experiences and deliver your brand promise. I like to think of the ideal customer archetype as the profile of that single customer who will spend the most money with you over the longest time because he or she has so strongly bought into your brand experience.

The reason why this chapter is titled "This Is Not a Shoe" is because we are going to talk about two companies that do a lot of things right in their branding and have grown exponentially as a result. Both companies happen to be in the shoe business. The first brand is Zappos.com, an e-commerce retailer of shoes and accessories. But in branding terms, Zappos is not a shoe company; Zappos is a relationship company. I'll explain why in this chapter.

We will also talk about Nike. While Nike also sells shoes, the Nike brand is not entirely about shoes. The Nike brand is about creating an inner dialogue with the athlete inside of every person. Companies that do branding well are much more than just the products they sell. They represent transcendent ideas; they tell stories about their users.

## ZAPPOS IS A RELATIONSHIP COMPANY

I have an emotional connection to the Zappos brand. I know this sounds really dorky, but I'm absolutely obsessed. Zappos is a customer service company that just happens to sell shoes. I feel so strongly about the Zappos brand, and I believe in them so much, that if Zappos decided that they were going to sell power tools and I needed a pneumatic wrench for my garage, Zappos would be the first place I would shop.

I've been tracking my order history with Zappos for more than 10 years. One of the things I noticed, because I'm very quantitatively oriented, is that, over time, not only did my order frequency consistently increase, but the size of those orders also increased. The more I got to know Zappos, and the more I started buying from Zappos, I found that it really enhanced the story of my life—and that made me buy even more.

It's kind of a head scratcher when you think about it, because there are many more direct and immediate ways for me to purchase shoes right here in Austin, Texas. In fact, there is a really nice Nordstrom store right down the road. I could walk in there at any moment, see a pair of shoes I like, put them on my feet, hand over my credit card, and walk out of the store wearing them. But with Zappos, I have to wait a full 24 hours to get a pair of shoes.

That seems ludicrous, right? Well, that's the essence of irrational loyalty as we discussed in chapter one.

Sure, I can buy shoes at Nordstrom or any other brick-and-mortar retailer in town. However, the shopping experiences at those places don't make me feel as good as what I feel when I shop at Zappos. Not only did my order frequency and average order size increase steadily over the past 10 years, but the rate at which I returned purchases increased too. As a pioneer of the free returns policy for online purchases, Zappos gives everyone free returns.

If you remember, there was a time when people were not willing to throw down their credit card to buy items online because they worried that if they didn't like them, or they weren't the right size, or they didn't fit right, they would feel remorse. And then returning those items would be a huge hassle. You probably remember that in the early days of e-commerce, the process of going to the post office or UPS store and packaging and sending a return was absolutely soul crushing, not to mention expensive.

Zappos looked to its customers to understand the causes of friction in the relationships customers had with e-commerce retailers. They learned that one of the most significant barriers to online purchases was the hassle surrounding returns. So, with the wave of a magic wand, Zappos eliminated it. This was the first in a series of moves that transformed an online shoe seller into an e-commerce leader by making customer service and the Zappos brand experience, not margins, first priority. Zappos is customer obsessed, and it shows in every dealing I have with them: from the simple and intuitive shopping interface to how they notify me when out-of-stock items I've looked at come back in stock to their unflinching openness to my returning hundreds of purchases a year.

The Zappos customer service culture is so strong that they've built their brand on it. The Zappos culture is so legendary that they run a Zappos "culture camp" for companies looking to emulate that culture in their own businesses. I know companies, actual clients of mine, who have sent their CEOs and their COOs and customer service leaders to Las Vegas to learn the Zappos way.

## EIGHT PAIRS OF SHOES FOR NEW YEAR'S EVE

Zappos's commitment to customer service definitely pays off in my case. I believe that their free return policy not only removes a significant purchase barrier, but it encourages me to buy more from them. When I was in New York over this past Christmas, I decided on a particular dress for an upcoming New Year's Eve celebration.

This little black dress, while not particularly hot, could become something else entirely with the right footwear. So I wanted to wear a pair of brightly colored shoes with the dress, and I wanted them to be really, really hot. So right from the comfort of my New York friend's kitchen counter, I got on Zappos.com, and I bought not just one pair of shoes, but eight. I thought to myself, "I need to see each pair with this dress, and then I'll pick one and return the other seven, because returns are free."

I put seven gorgeous (and expensive) pairs of shoes in my basket, clicked "order," and had an order confirmation in my e-mail inbox before you could say "Salvatore Ferragamo." Those eight luscious pairs of shoes showed up on my doorstep at about the same time I arrived back home in Texas. In that Zappos box, I had eight pairs of shoes to try on in the comfort of my own home, with my dress, my jewelry, and seven different experimental hairstyles. Expecting to find the one perfect pair of shoes, I ended up with three. My purchase of three pairs of shoes ended up being pretty substantial for Zappos. That multiple pair purchase probably wouldn't have happened at a traditional retailer, and it for sure wouldn't have happened had I known that I was going to be charged for shipping both ways. Zappos's obsession with customer service paid off for not only me, but for the company as well.

The point I'm trying to make here is that when your story is not just the product you sell, when it's the total experience customers have with your brand, you can forge very powerful and profitable relationships. So at Zappos, a shoe is a shoe. They aren't the brand; they're just what gives you access to the Zappos brand experience.

## IDEAL CUSTOMERS SPEND MORE

As I said before, I've been tracking my Zappos order history for years. In fact, every year I publish a post on my blog that includes a chart indicating order frequency, order volume, order price, and order returns. I plot these out and measure increases year over year. When you look at these graphs, you can see that over the lifetime of my relationship with Zappos, I purchased more each time I ordered; I ordered more, increasingly expensive items; I returned more; I kept more; and I spent more overall. From Zappos's perspective, I am their ideal customer. I am bonded with them for life.

Zappos eliminates the things that I don't like about shopping at the mall, which include everything from getting in my car and driving in Austin traffic, competing for a parking spot, subjecting myself to annoying sales associates, dealing with limited selection at the physical store, waiting in line to check out to stopping at Mrs. Fields for a half-dozen chocolate chip cookies, and so on. When you think about it, making *returns* at the mall isn't a cakewalk either. You have to go through all of the aforementioned steps and deal with a snarky sales associate who likely just lost her commission. With Zappos, returns are as easy as handing a box to my UPS guy when he comes to the office. Simple.

I'm totally Zappos's ideal customer. You probably can't guess how much I spend with Zappos in an average year. I'm embarrassed to say it. In a typical year, I will spend about $15,000 with Zappos. Wait, did I just admit that publicly? But I'll easily return about 25 percent of that. On the odd chance that Zappos is out of stock on an item I really want, I might be disappointed, but I'll still keep coming back, because, ultimately, I feel the Zappos love. There's so much love built up between Zappos and me that the company can disappoint me, and I'll keep coming back.

Here's the key point about identifying your ideal customer. If Zappos spent all of its efforts branding for their ideal customers, like me, they'd be wildly successful. Even if customers like me only represent 20 percent of their customer base, we'd probably make up about 80 percent of their revenue.

Thinking about the profile of your ideal customer gives

you a very clear picture of the person for whom you are creating the brand. And it's likely that 80 percent of your customers are not going to fit that ideal customer profile exactly—maybe they spend less, or shop less frequently, or use your brand for a purpose that's an alternative to your brand's intended use. But knowing who that customer is and what moves him or her will help you answer the question, "Who is our brand ultimately for?" Having an ideal customer in mind brings focus to all of your branding efforts.

## HOW TO IDENTIFY THE IDEAL CUSTOMER

How do you identify your ideal customer? First, talk to as many existing customers as you possibly can, either through formal or informal research (I think my next book will be about customer insights and how to get them on the cheap.). You'll want to know everything you can from them about their experiences with your brand as well as other key characteristics we'll get into in a bit.

If you don't have access to a research budget, or methods for conducting extensive, statistically-validated research, then do what we in the biz call "mother-in-law research." You can conduct this kind of research informally as you move through your regular life. Use your social channels. If your mother-in-law is a customer, call her up and ask her questions. Of course, it's not ideal, because your friends and family (even your in-laws) want to see you be successful in your business endeavors. Beware of false positives from well-meaning contacts. Make sure when you ask your personal network for input that you remind them to be as candid as possible and to leave their personal feelings about you aside.

After you've spoken to enough customers and people in your social networks who use the product, try to write down a description of your ideal customer. Now this is where the creative part comes in. Close your eyes and conjure up a vivid image of who the perfect person is to buy your brand. Who is that person? How old is that person? Is the person male or female? Married or single? What is the person's age, income, and so on? Conjure up an image of who that person is, and write down everything you can think of.

First think demographically, and then try to imagine his or her lifestyle. For instance, for a hypothetical online grocer in the Northeast, the ideal customer might be a 35-year-old mom with two school-age kids at home, who works 30 hours a week outside of the home. She lives in the New York suburbs. She shops for groceries once a week in a big shopping trip, and then she does fill-in shopping every other day. She's a technology user; she has a smartphone and a laptop and a tablet. She wears high-end casual clothes with designer labels when she shops. She carries a gigantic pocketbook. She keeps a yoga mat in her expensive European SUV, and she does not like minivans. Her total household income is around $200,000. Go through the process of envisioning who this person is. Write it all down. Even draw a picture of her if you have to.

This is the profile of your ideal customer, that one customer you're creating this brand for and for whom you can be everything. Can you get a picture of who this person is with just that description?

Now, use your imagination to dial in your vision of this customer even further. Imagine her getting out of her SUV wearing one of her two or three pairs of high-end designer jeans that cost around $200. Her entire wardrobe isn't that, but she has a couple pairs of those jeans because she does value the finer things. She's wearing a puffy down vest that is probably from the North Face brand because that's what all the other moms are wearing when they pick up their kids from private school.

Think about what we can surmise about this customer from the description you created. We know that she values form and function and style. But also, we know that both she and her husband work, and they have those busy kids, so they don't have a ton of free time. This woman, this customer, has a self concept she's looking to elevate through the brands she uses and a message she wants to send to other people. Both influence her brand and buying choices.

Going through this exercise helps you gain clarity about who your ideal customer is on both the outside and, more importantly, the inside. Once you get really specific on that vision of the ideal customer, you'll know more about what she values and what she believes. When you think about the other brands she surrounds herself with and the other types of products she values and the stories that she's telling about herself with those products, you start to understand even more.

That's the first step in determining the ideal customer archetype—really dialing in this visual picture of who that person is. Remember when doing this exercise, always think about the person who is most highly predictive of success for this brand. This is not just any customer, but the person who is going to be in the top 20 percent of users of this brand.

Note: Creating an ideal customer profile isn't just for brands with an existing customer set. If you're in startup mode, you can still do the ideal customer archetype exercise. Go through the same steps to identify who would be the customer most highly predictive of your success—that one customer who would be "perfect" for your brand and for whom your brand would be ideal.

## IDENTIFY THE IDEAL CUSTOMER'S NEEDS

After you've taken that first step of creating a picture of that ideal customer, go to step two—think about that person's needs. This is the hardest part of the ideal customer archetype process. This is the part where you have to really dig in.

Before, in the grocery example, I created a picture of this suburban, working mom with two kids. From that detailed description, I can probably deduce some of her needs. She needs to feel like she is the best possible parent she can be. She also needs to look like the best parent in comparison to other moms at her kids' school. Since she works outside the home, she likely feels the strain of balancing her job and spending time with her kids at this critical age. So she has needs for activities and services and products that give her as much time as possible to spend with her kids in the way that she wants to that also makes her feel like she is fulfilling her potential as their mom.

We also know that she values quality in the products that she buys because she doesn't have time to drive around town making returns. In thinking about food, for instance, she probably wants to have the healthiest, most nutritious meals she can get for her children without the need to do a lot of shopping or preparation. She certainly doesn't have time to shop at multiple grocery stores, and sometimes she doesn't have the time to cook everything that comes to the table for a family meal. However, she still wants to feel like she's the provider of tonight's dinner and that the meal meets her very high standards. Remember when we talked about answering the question, "How do we make the customer the hero in his or her own story?" Well, defining the ideal customers' needs helps you do exactly that.

## MAKE THIS A GROUP ACTIVITY

The ideal customer archetype exercise is ideally done in a group brainstorming session with the staff in your company who are most involved in customer-facing roles. But don't just invite the top executives. Often it's your salespeople, customer service reps, returns processors, and delivery drivers who are closest to the customers. They actually know more about your customers than your marketing team ever could.

Understanding your ideal customer in depth enables you

to understand what that person needs most from you and your brand. The ideal customer archetype exercise empowers you to match your brand promise and your brand experience to those specific needs. So in summary, you start by thinking about exactly who this person is and then dial in their demographics—what they look, think, and act like, as well as what brands they value and love. Then you take that detailed description and extract from it the story that the customer wants to tell about him or herself. Eventually you'll get a clear image of who your ideal customer is and, ultimately, whom your brand is for.

Companies often struggle with these branding exercises because it's hard to leave behind the myths and beliefs that are part of the company history. It can be difficult to change your perspective on your ideal customer when a different customer has been part of the company's tribal knowledge. Whenever you become sharper with your focus and more precise about who you are for and what you promise to them, you have to give up some old ideas. That's hard. Ultimately, this ideal customer process is extremely galvanizing for companies.

## THE BUTCHER PAPER EXERCISE

It's galvanizing because it brings people together. The following example will demonstrate how. One of the companies that I worked with for a long time was iVillage.com. Back in its heyday, iVillage was probably the largest online destination for women. At the time I started working with the company, it had just become part of NBC Universal. With a mid-2000s onslaught of "mom media," iVillage struggled to remain relevant and knew it had to reinvent itself in order to compete. Additionally, the proliferation of highly focused digital media sites in passion verticals, such as food, entertainment, parenting, fashion, and beauty, was stealing their readers. By late 2011, iVillage was struggling to figure out how to both narrow its focus and grow traffic. As part of a branding engagement, I had them do the ideal customer exercise.

The ideal customer archetype exercise is one of the things I love about my job. The engagement at iVillage was no exception. For iVillage's ideal customer exercise, my team brought out a big roll of butcher paper and cut it into six-foot lengths. We divided up the staff of about 100 employees into smaller groups. We gave each group markers, art supplies, magazines, photographs, glue, and scissors. Then I gave them the assignment of creating an image of iVillage's ideal customer, using all that stuff.

One group actually had one of their team members lay down on the butcher paper, and they traced her body with magic marker. They gave her big eyes and big ears because they wanted to communicate, "Our ideal customer is somebody who has a curiosity about the world around her and is seeking information from other people."

Another group drew their ideal customer as a woman with a gigantic pocketbook filled with items from different categories, such as parenting, beauty, fashion, and health. Their idea was, "Our ideal customer is somebody who is super engaged and productive in her world and needs inspiration, information, and connections in all of these different areas of her life." Another group drew this Picassoesque Cubist version of a woman with five arms and six legs and 10 eyes. This was their version of a woman who is doing a lot of things at once.

Each team presented their ideal customer diagrams to the rest of the teams. Then I challenged them as a larger group to combine those traits to come up with a singular ideal customer profile. That group of 100 people used all of those inputs to create the North Star version of their ideal customer. That's extremely galvanizing to a team, especially when they went through that physical process of drawing and cutting and pasting and gluing and then presenting, persuading, and narrowing their focus to eventually align on a singular profile.

The point of this exercise is that the company must conduct an in-depth examination of what ideal customers need from its brand. A shared vision of the ideal customer is very powerful.

## YOUR BRAND PROMISE

When you think about the promise you make to this ideal customer, you have to ascend to the top of the brand values pyramid. The brand promise is the combination of everything in that brand values pyramid. "Yes, we meet all of the table stakes minimum requirements. Yes, we have some interesting bells and whistles that provide functional and emotional advantages. But, most importantly, we answer those three big questions at the top of the pyramid." At the top of the pyramid are those self-expressive benefits that make the customer feel, "You understand me, and your values as a brand align with mine. I'm your ideal customer."

The stuff at the top of the pyramid for Zappos is what they call "wow." For Zappos, that's their obsession with customer service: their ability to empower me to be the most stylish and most fashionable I can be and to give me what I need to tell the story of my life through what I wear on my feet.

## ALLRECIPES VERSUS EPICURIOUS

One of the brands we talked about earlier was Allrecipes. com, which at its core is an online recipe website. When I started working with them back in 2006, their major competition came from other recipe sites such as Food-Network.com and Epicurious.com. Google was emerging as a threat to direct-to-site web traffic and brand loyalty because they offered functionality that allowed users to type in some ingredients and get a list of recipes from sites across the Internet. To most people, cookbooks were becoming a thing of the past. The deep existential question Allrecipes asked itself was, "Who is this brand for, and how do we carve out a unique role and remain relevant?" The answer to this question lies in their exploration of the ideal customer archetype.

My company started at Allrecipes by identifying their ideal customer, what that ideal customer needed from Allrecipes, and what Allrecipes's promise was to them. At its core, Allrecipes isn't just an online recipe database. Allrecipes solves a multitude of cooking-related problems for consumers. With hundreds of thousands of user-generated and kitchen-tested recipes, a full suite of technique videos, special recipe collections designed to ease decision making and speed preparation, and ratings, reviews, and photographs, the Allrecipes brand is about making home cooks feel a sense of accomplishment in the kitchen. Allrecipes likes to express its purpose for every-day home cooks as answering the question, "What's for dinner tonight?" That is what's at the top of the Allrecipes brand values pyramid.

When you walk through the Allrecipes brand values pyra-mid, you see that they satisfy all the baseline requirements for any recipe website. They have some exciting attributes in the middle tier of the pyramid—hundreds of thou-sands of user-created recipes that have been reviewed and commented on by other users and vetted and tested in Allrecipes kitchens. They have a unique search by ingredient function that excludes certain ingredients if that's what the user wants. Allrecipes also has specific recipe collections addressing seasonal ingredients, holi-day themes, and even answers to the question, "Chicken again?" They have a mobile app customers can use while shopping for groceries so they can plan out meals with ingredients on sale in the store. They have technique videos viewed over 100 million times in an average year. So when you get to the top of the Allrecipes pyramid, the company ultimately provides home cooks with a sense of accomplishment in the kitchen and an answer to the question, "What's for dinner tonight?"

Allrecipes gives everyday home cooks a sense of accom-plishment from knowing, "This is a fail-safe recipe that's been tested. All the reviewers loved it. I am going to be able to do this. Another mom like me contributed it. And 400 other moms with suggestions for substitutions or ways to make it lighter have reviewed it." Additionally, because of the fact that a recipe's been submitted by someone just like them and kitchen tested at Allrecipes or prepared successfully by 400 other moms, these home cooks know it works. That feeling of confidence and accomplishment that customers get from Allrecipes is at the top of their brand values pyramid. It's impossible to duplicate. That's how Allrecipes has really differentiated itself and created a very clear promise to inspire home cooks with confidence that they can make a great meal not just on a special occasion, but any day of the week.

In comparison, consider Epicurious.com. It's also a recipe site. You could argue that it competes with Allrecipes because both sites provide recipes. But the top of the Epicurious brand values pyramid is completely different from Allrecipes's. Epicurious.com is beautiful. It's upscale. It's all about in-depth editorial and gorgeous, professional photography. It's about gourmet meals, exotic ingredients, and advanced techniques. The brand is about special occasions and entertaining and impressing others. Epicurious is a site specifically for foodies, not everyday home cooks. Cooks who prepare an Epicurious recipe get to wear a symbolic badge of honor for tackling a recipe with an average of forty different ingredients. Cooks who make a meal using a recipe on Epicurious are expressing their creativity and challenging themselves through cooking. The Epicurious ideal customer probably wants to impress somebody else on a special occasion instead of answering the everyday home cook question, "What's for dinner tonight?"

If you take Epicurious and Allrecipes and compare them to each other, the two sites meet the same baseline requirements. They both have huge, searchable recipe databases. They both have photographs of finished meals. They have reviews from other cooks. They have methods to scale recipes to larger and smaller audiences. The recipes are vetted and tested. Both sites meet the basic requirements for any business calling itself a "recipe site."

However, where the brands diverge is in the middle and top tiers of their brand values pyramids. Each site has different features that differentiate them and make them meaningful to their ideal customers. For instance, Epicurious has an entire section of the website dedicated to "expert advice," while Allrecipes communicates to the world that it's the "world's largest food-focused social network, focusing on 'food, friends, and fun,'" and features recipes and photographs submitted by home cooks, not professionals. Epicurious's brand focuses on delivering original content written by their own editors and leading food authorities around the world. Each of the two brands solves similar problems for consumers, but they built their brands for different ideal customers.

At the top of the brand values pyramid is the ultimate promise you make to your ideal customer. What you're really selling is a relationship and an experience. Nike is an example of another company that does this really well.

## NIKE: JUST BRAND IT

Nike is a huge company with multiple product lines. It has Nike Golf. It has running. It has football. It has sportswear. It even sells technology designed to improve your workout. It has products for professional athletes, and it has products for recreational athletes like you and me. It's interesting that across all of the product lines that the company sells to a wide variety of people, the Nike brand remains consistent.

The top of Nike's brand values pyramid are values and beliefs the company addresses for its ideal customer. What customers have in common across all of the company's product lines is a belief that there is an athlete inside each and every one of them. I've heard that Nike sometimes expresses this as, "If you have a body, you are an athlete." Nike's brand speaks directly to everyone's inner athlete and stimulates an inspiring internal dialogue that customers have with themselves. The "Just Do It" brand and advertising campaign has always been good at being *about* the person who's using the Nike brand rather than the products themselves. The inspiring internal dialogue that each and every customer has with his or her inner athlete is at the core of the relationship customers have with the Nike brand.

Really strong and consistent brands that have nailed their ideal customer profile, such as Nike, can extend into many product lines. The Nike brand resonates through all of its product lines, whether the actual buyer is a high school athletic director, a soccer mom, or an elite professional marathoner. Inside the company, everybody who touches and interacts with the brand is a steward of the brand. That's an attitude and a philosophy that starts from high up within the organization. CEOs who believe in the power of branding and make stewarding the brand part of the culture often lead companies with really strong brands.

## BRAND ARCHETYPES

Many people think of branding as this squishy, touchy-feely pursuit. Some people have a hard time wrapping their minds around branding and how a brand is designed to have meaning in customers' own stories. A trick we use as brand strategists is to inspire brands to think of themselves as a human being playing a particular role in a customer's story—a brand archetype. Thinking of your brand as an iconic human archetype can make some of the squishier concepts feel more concrete.

The idea of brand archetypes comes from a 2001 book entitled *The Hero and The Outlaw* by Margaret Mack. I highly recommend that branding enthusiasts read this book. According to the book, there are 12 master story-telling archetypes: the outlaw, the explorer, the creator, the hero, the magician, the sage, the ruler, the innocent, the everyman, the caregiver, the lover, and the jester. They're classic character types you recognize from stories, movies, and books.

These archetypal characters are in the Bible. They're in *Star Wars*. They're in *Harry Potter*. They're in *The Lord of the Rings*. They're in television commercials. They're in popular contemporary fiction. They're in classic fiction. You can even see these archetypes in history.

**BRAND Archetypes**

HOW TO PLAY AN IMPORTANT ROLE IN YOUR CUSTOMER'S STORY

**THE MAGICIAN**

I MAKE THINGS HAPPEN

CORE DESIRE:
understanding the fundamental laws of the universe
GOAL: to make dreams come true

**THE SAGE**

THE TRUTH WILL SET YOU FREE

CORE DESIRE:
to find the truth
GOAL: to use intelligence and analysis to understand the world

**THE INNOCENT**

FREE TO BE YOU AND ME

CORE DESIRE:
to get to paradise
GOAL: to be happy

**THE OUTLAW**

RULES ARE MADE TO BE BROKEN

CORE DESIRE:
revenge or revolution
GOAL: to overturn what isn't working

**THE JESTER**

YOU ONLY LIVE ONCE

CORE DESIRE:
to live in the moment with full enjoyment
GOAL: to have a great time and lighten up the world

**THE LOVER**

YOU'RE THE ONLY ONE

CORE DESIRE:
intimacy and experience
GOAL: a relationship with the people, work and surroundings they love

### THE EXPLORER

DON'T FENCE ME IN

CORE DESIRE:
the freedom to find out who you are through exploring the world
GOAL: to experience a better, more authentic, more fulfilling life

### THE RULER

POWER ISN'T EVERYTHING, IT'S THE ONLY THING

CORE DESIRE:
control
GOAL: create a prosperous, successful family or community

### THE CAREGIVER

LOVE YOUR NEIGHBOR AS YOURSELF

CORE DESIRE:
to protect and care for others
GOAL: to help others

### THE HERO

WHERE THERE'S A WILL, THERE'S A WAY

CORE DESIRE:
to prove one's worth through courageous acts
GOAL: expert mastery in a way that improves the world

### THE REGULAR GUY/GIRL

ALL MEN AND WOMEN ARE CREATED EQUAL

CORE DESIRE:
connecting with others
GOAL: to belong

### THE CREATOR

IF YOU CAN IMAGINE IT, IT CAN BE DONE

CORE DESIRE:
to create things of enduring value
GOAL: to realize a vision

Every brand could be one of these archetypes. For example, the outlaw represents brands that break the rules, live outside the bounds of normal society, and don't care what civilized society thinks. The outlaw is the ultimate in freedom. This is a good archetype for brands that are trying to disrupt an industry or revolutionize something or disobey the rules. They want to upset the status quo. A very famous outlaw brand to me would be Harley Davidson. Some people also consider Apple to be an outlaw brand.

A brand aligned with the jester archetype is about enjoying life and living in the moment. One of our Sol Marketing clients with a jester brand is the digital media company called Cheezburger. Cheezburger's brand is all about bringing "five minutes of funny" into somebody's life.

Sage brands are intelligent and erudite. Explorer brands are about going off the beaten path and finding your own way. Lover brands are about intimacy, showing appreciation, and demonstrating commitment. The everyman archetype is about common, ordinary wants and needs and simple pleasures. You get the idea.

So I recommend you choose one of these 12 classic archetypes that best fits your brand, because it's convenient and can make branding easier for some people inside your organization to understand. Sometimes when clients are struggling with the concept of a brand's archetype, I give them the shortcut of thinking about iconic movie characters or even celebrities. I'll often say, "Think about your favorite movies. What movie character is most like your brand?" For example, the actor Tom Hanks is the classic everyman archetype.

Interestingly, when I walk through this methodology with clients and ask, "Which archetype is your brand?" nearly 100 percent of the time they say they want to be the everyman archetype. This is perhaps because companies are afraid to choose for fear that they may leave some customer behind. I'll tell you this: unless you're Folgers Coffee, it's unlikely I'm going to let your brand be the everyman archetype. In today's product and service saturated world, branding requires you to be highly meaningful to a customer who is most highly predictive of your success, not just semi-meaningful to all customers. Yes, choice is hard, but it always leads to greater focus.

## FIND YOUR BRAND PERSONALITY

Once you've determined your brand archetype, next you can assign a brand personality. The brand personality can help bring your brand into clearer focus. It provides you with clues to how you want customers to experience your brand—the feeling you want to give them when they interact with you through your marketing, customer service, and even your products.

To understand your brand's personality, think again of your brand as if it were a human being. Create a comprehensive list of personality traits by detailing as many characteristics of that person as you can. If you're having trouble getting started, begin by considering how old your brand is. Is it 10 years old? Is it 20 years old? Is it 40 years old? Is it 65 years old? Is your brand a man or a woman? Is it friendly or slightly more aggressive? Is it a lone wolf? Is it funny? Is it maybe a little bit irreverent? Does it like to shock people?

One of my favorite travel brands is Virgin America. I will happily fly at odd times of the day or on different days of the week in order to take a Virgin flight instead of a flight on one of the usual suspects—United, American, or Delta—just because I love the Virgin brand. When you think about it, most of our domestic airlines are explorer brands and have really dry, authoritarian personalities (with the exception of Southwest Airlines). Aside from going "off book" as an outlaw brand, the Virgin brand personality is distinctly different from other airlines. It's upbeat. It's funny. It's uplifting. It's irreverent. It doesn't feel oppressive and rigid like the other airlines.

Most travel days, I show up at the airport thinking, "How am I going to get screwed today?" When I fly Virgin, I don't have that feeling, and I actually look forward to flying. When I fly Virgin, I feel the brand's warmth. It's welcoming. It's modern. It's hip. It's lighthearted. In contrast, I recently took a trip to New York on Delta, another brand that offers a product that is exactly the same as what Virgin America provides. Yet Delta's personality feels completely different than Virgin's. Everything on Delta was totally buttoned up, all the way down to the uniforms that the flight attendants wore—pressed blouses buttoned all the way up to the top, suit jackets and vests, and black stockings. To Delta's credit, they had an entertaining in-flight safety video featuring a host of visual gags to keep passengers' attention. But the whole experience of watching that video fell flat because it didn't align with the rest of Delta's more serious brand personality.

Brand personality is so important for defining the way people experience the brand, to the essence of the brand, all the way down to the creative articulation of the brand. The brand personality informs everything from the way the brand looks, the way it sounds, the voice and music beds it uses in its commercials, the actual words it always says, and words it would never say. Brand personality is another way to ensure your brand carries the right tone and character to deliver on your brand promise to your customer.

Doug Guller owns a sports bar and grill chain called Bikinis USA, which bills itself as the nation's only Breastaraunt®. I am a middle-aged mom who generally reacts negatively to businesses that objectify women. However, as a student of branding and an admirer of gutsy marketing campaigns, I'm a big fan of how Bikinis started a crazy love affair with its customers. The company offered a $100 Bikinis bar tab to customers who would get a permanent tattoo of the Bikinis "B" logo somewhere on their bodies—and Bikinis would pay for the tattoo. More than 180 Bikinis customers got the tattoo. Now *that* is irrational loyalty.

**Where did this idea come from?**
My team came up with the campaign. I didn't think anyone would do it—but the team assured me that we would have a few people. If a few people wanted to do it, it was worth it. I was shocked at the response. Backs and arms. A few ankles. A Bikini waistline. That was, of course, a woman.

**What did customers get in exchange for having a capital Bikinis "B" indelibly etched on their bodies for eternity?**
The exchange was that 1) we paid for it, and 2) we gave them a $100 gift card to their local Bikinis. Interestingly, for something to be branded on them for the rest of their lives, we were only out of pocket for about $200—and $100 of that was in trade!

**How did the campaign affect the Bikinis brand?**

What we generally go for is the feeling of making people smile or laugh. We don't take ourselves too seriously. Our value proposition is our service and our food. As you know, we call ourselves a "Breastaurant." To be in that space, you can't take yourself too seriously. You have to offer something to the general public that is light hearted. When we go for our PR stunts, we generally want to put a smile on people's faces and get them to laugh out loud. The Bikinis world is very polarizing. It draws a response right away. When we do this kind of branding campaign, it's for people to say "Oh, they're at it again."

**So what kinds of people tattoo a logo on their bodies in exchange for perks?**

That's a hard question to answer. I met some down here in Austin the day of the event. They are frequent customers or "fans" of Bikinis. They were all male. The girls who got them were all employees who have all been with us for a while. They are all excited about the brand. They have a sense of belonging. They know us; they have made a lot of friends by sitting around the bar over the years.

**What does it say about people that they are hardcore fans of Bikinis, or that they have a big blue "B" tattooed on their arms?**

It says they want a sense of belonging to some kind of brand or tribe or group. They are usually sports enthusiasts. This fits in with their personal tastes.

We focus on four things: food, booze, sex, and sports. Our fans generally love one of those or all four of those things. They want to be a part of something bigger than themselves.

**What were you trying to achieve from is tattoo campaign?**
We wanted to give our really excited fans something they wanted, and I wanted to see where our brand could go. When I started this seven years ago, I didn't realize people would be so into us that they'd have a "B" permanently marked on their bodies for the rest of their lives!

**What will you do next?**
We are doing a big contest called "Miss Bikinis USA." It will be very different from a beauty pageant; ours will be more "Fun Factor meets Texas Hill Country." We'll have girls shooting guns and doing a variety of fun things, eating things they don't want to, stuff like that. This kind of pageant fits with our brand of not taking ourselves too seriously. Fans will love it.

**What are your key takeaways from this experience?**
It's been about pushing the limits and putting ourselves out there and being vulnerable to people criticizing us. My advice: if you feel confident in your brand, and you realize you only have one life to live—go for it. There's no reason not to. As long as you feel like it will advance your brand, then it's great. We always think, "How is this different than what everyone else is doing?" That's our litmus test. A lot of restaurants don't have the kind of following we do. That's why we are traveling down this road.

*SEVEN*

# THE BULLSHIT TEST

**CONGRATULATIONS.** You've made it to the final chapter of the book. At this point, you've identified and profiled your ideal customer. You built the foundation of your brand values pyramid. You also know what's at the top of the pyramid. And you've answered those three deep existential branding questions. So are you done? Um... no.

You are never done branding. You always need to stay in touch with your customers, because people, market forces, demographics, and needs change. When we talk about customers, we're not talking about single-cell amoebas here. We're talking about extremely complex individuals who use your brand as a way to elevate their self concept. And as new brands enter the market and create innovative ways of addressing customer needs, customers' expectations change. When you don't stay in touch with your customers, they'll call "bullshit" on you.

## BRANDING NEVER ENDS

If you have children, I'm sure they've asked you to read the same book over and over and over again. I can hear my daughter now, "Again, again, Mommy." I think the book she loved was *Goodnight Moon.* "Again, again, Mommy." That story had an end, and it always ended the same. But if branding is a story, it's the story that never ends.

With all brands, circumstances change. Branding is an ongoing exercise in defining and redefining yourself. Remember the story of FreshDirect? The company's marketplace and competitive environment underwent massive change in just a few short years. If it wasn't involved in the practice of continually refining its brand, the company would be screwed.

It would never be able to keep up with the changes in its marketplace and keep its brand relevant in introducing new services, products, and delivery options. Smartly, FreshDirect stays in constant touch with its customers' changing needs. That means continually reaching out to those customers for insights, both formally and informally, as well as keeping an eye on its market.

## STAY OUT OF THE BRAND GRAVEYARD

When you slack off at branding, you stop paying attention, which allows room for someone to emerge out of nowhere and sucker punch you right in your market share.

Do you think I'm exaggerating? Ha! Think about all the once-powerful brands that are now dead and buried in what I call the brand graveyard. Pontiac, Max Factor, Hummer, MCI Worldcom, First Boston, Montgomery Ward, Howard Johnson's, EF Hutton, Paine Webber, Enron, Eastern Airlines, Lionel Trains, Compaq, Chemical Bank, Plymouth, Kinney Shoes, Burger Chef, Pan Am Airlines, Burdines, DeLorean, Arthur Andersen, Merry-Go-Round, TWA, Marshall Fields, Bonwit Teller, Rustler Steak House, and GTE are but a few.

And don't forget the classic graveyard brand, Kodak. What the heck happened to Kodak? Your instinct might be to blurt out, "Digital photography killed Kodak." Well, yes and no. I'll tell you what happened to Kodak: they lost touch with their customers. If Kodak had stayed on top of their customers' needs and wants, they would have seen the tidal wave of digital coming and could have potentially remained relevant in a filmless world. Although they were actually (ironically) the inventor of the digital camera, they were never able to connect with customers on a relevant level. During the initial digital photography wave, Kodak doubled down on the chemical processes used in making film, while upstart technology disruptors such as Sony and Canon shook up the industry and successfully made film nearly obsolete.

Asking the three brand questions may have guided Kodak to place more focus on digital photography and to evolve their existing brand story to become about instantly capturing memories and living the fun in an instant—instead of remaining steeped in a story about archiving life's most precious memories on film. With proper brand management, Kodak might have been able to successfully foray into digital photography and maybe even emerge as a leader in digital imaging. Kodak filed Chapter 11 in 2012. The company's legacy attachment to film likely blinded it to real consumer opportunities in the digital world.

## PAY ATTENTION TO YOUR CUSTOMERS

The cautionary tale of Kodak makes me think of an analogy about something good storytellers do. When I first moved to Austin, Texas, the Whole Foods store in downtown Austin used to host a weekly story hour for kids. Every couple of weeks, I would take my kid and we'd sit and listen to some hippy tell a wild story or read the politically correct children's book of the moment. Actually, for children and parents alike, it was the pinnacle of storytelling. These were some of the most talented storytellers I'd ever seen.

The storytellers usually were some folksy people who, on the surface, didn't look like brain surgeons. But something happened as soon as they started telling their stories. They became animated and energetic. They made eye contact with all of the kids in the audience. A lot. As I watched my kid sitting cross-legged in front of the storytellers, I could see she would sit up pin straight when the storyteller made eye contact with her. She would perk up, lean forward, smile, and her eyes would get big and shine with the light of a thousand suns.

By making eye contact with the kids in the audience, the storytellers could constantly judge how the audience was reacting to the story. Great public speakers and politicians do the same thing. If the speaker senses the audience is getting bored or restless, he can adjust the pace of the story. He can adjust his volume, facial expressions, and hand gestures. He can see when people are straining to hear him. He can also sense when he's being too loud or too soft. When the audience is not getting the message, the storyteller can give them more of whatever they need to bond them more closely to the story.

That's a great analogy for what companies need to do with their customers. Look them in the eyes and gauge their reaction to your brand. Companies can do this by meeting with customers and talking to them face-to-face about the brand. All companies need to have a process for going out and staying in touch with and engaged with their audience through formal and informal insight gathering.

## INDISPENSABILITY AND SINGULARITY

Indispensability and singularity are critical to your brand's long-term success. But you will never know if you are indispensable to your customers if you don't ask them. Brands that rest on their laurels and think that their singularity lives somewhere in the middle tier of the pyramid or exclusively in their products and services are brands that will lose. Kodak is a great example of this.

Now think about enduring brands that have evolved and remained indispensable for decades. The Apple brand, for instance, has been around for most of our lifetime. I actually remember our first Apple IIe computer at home. I was probably in junior high at the time.

Apple's brand has evolved, and its products have evolved. The company has created new categories and new product lines. By staying in constant, close contact with their customers, Apple has remained indispensable and relevant to its users. In the years since the Apple IIe, the company has introduced the Macintosh, created a whole new category with the iPod, and successfully combined telecommunications and handheld computing in a single device with the iPhone, all with the same overarching purpose of introducing innovative technology to simplify our lives. Many Apple customers would argue that Apple has made itself indispensable to them by doing so.

Most people don't know the story of Nokia. Nokia was once the world's largest manufacturer of cell phones. But long before that, Nokia was a producer of rubber boots. True story! Yes, rubber boots. Well-known across the world for their useful features and groundbreaking comfort, Nokia Kontio boots were the gold standard for protective footwear in the 1970s and '80s in Europe and beyond.

In 1990, Nokia sold off its rubber boot division and went full force into communications technology. Seeing the needs of the marketplace change, Nokia turned to its customers to ask, "How can we take our core DNA of innovation and evolve our business so we can stay relevant, not only to the customers who currently embrace us but also to a whole new world of customers as they grow up?"

Soon Nokia was in the cell phone business. Now, as part of Alcatel-Lucent, they're leading a charge to use innovation to create technologies that connect people to one another. Last I heard, however, the glimmer of Kontio still glows within Nokia, and they're getting back into the rubber boot business. In 2014, they announced a deal with Microsoft to make "smart boots," promising calorie tracking, GPS navigation, mapping software synergies, gamified orienteering, and shoe-based social networks that revolve around mushroom picking and berry gathering.

If you want to find out how indispensable your brand is, go ask your customers. Ask them questions like, "If I took this brand away from you, what would your life be like?" If they say their lives would be significantly diminished in quality and joy because you took the brand away from them, you are indispensable. But if your customers answer, "Meh," you are not indispensable to them, and you had better figure out why.

If your customers feel they can live without your brand, then you are in a very precarious position. Or worse, if they indicate a desire to try something else, you're probably on your way out. You can ask these questions casually, or you can do it in a focus group. There are many different ways to do this, depending on your budget. But what I would recommend is walking in your customers' boots or calling them on the phone and asking them directly.

## FIVE CONVERSATIONS WITH CUSTOMERS EVERY WEEK

You don't have to hire a market research firm to talk to your customers. You can do it yourself quite effectively. In fact, I believe that every CEO of every company needs to have at least five conversations with customers every week. They can start by simply asking the three brand questions: What does it say about you that you use this brand? What is the one thing you get from us that you can't get from anyone else? How do we make you a hero? And if there's time, ask them about the state of their relationship with your brand and their satisfaction. Usually, you'll uncover all the problems you need to be aware of from just asking those questions.

If you're not talking to customers on a regular basis, you're taking your eye off the ball, and you could end up like Kodak, which is still trying to claw its way back from Chapter 11 bankruptcy. If the CEO doesn't have time to talk to customers, you do it. If you don't have time to do it, use your customer service people to ask those questions on a weekly basis. If your customer service people aren't able to ask customers questions, then use your customer service people as a proxy for your customers. It's not ideal, but it's something.

I always issue a word of caution to clients who are getting ready to have direct conversations with customers. First, be ready for answers you may not want to hear. When you've done right by your customers, they often don't say anything. But when your brand has done them wrong, be prepared for an earful. Asking deep questions of your customers can be like asking deep questions of a loved one like, "Do you still love me?" Seriously, don't ask the questions unless you are ready to hear the answer. That is why this process can cause soul searching and be a real gut check. Nevertheless, you must check in.

## THE BULLSHIT TEST

Branding is the process of defining and managing your relationship with your customers. When managing any kind of relationship, you don't just look to the other person. You also have to look within. As with interpersonal relationships, keeping your brand on good terms with customers often requires some self-examination. It's important to ask yourself if your organization is walking the walk and not just talking the talk about delivering on your brand promise. Maintaining brand integrity is paramount to ensuring the health of your brand relationships.

You need to make sure your organization delivers on your brand promise with every single customer touch point. Ask yourself, "Do we have places where it's an incomplete experience? Are our customer service representatives embodying what we say our brand stands for? Does our product or service really do what we say it does? Do customers experience the essence of our brand in a way that adds value to their lives?" It's important to know the answers to these questions so you can assess how well you and the rest of your organization are aligned on delivering a brand experience.

Remember the Zappos.com example from earlier? What if a customer called and had a problem with a pair of shoes and wanted some resolution but the customer service rep was snotty to her on the phone? That would be a place where the company was not fully delivering on the brand experience it promised.

Customers know when your brand messaging and your brand don't match. If the brand promises heroics, but then doesn't deliver, they'll cry, "Bullshit!" This means the brand messaging is bullshit, and customers can smell it a mile away. Don't fail the bullshit test. If you do, your customers may never come back.

## WHEN TO HIRE OUTSIDE HELP

One reason you may need professional help is that sometimes your boss or your team or your CEO is so in love with the brand that they can't see its flaws. Sometimes you need an outsider's perspective. It says on our Sol Marketing website, "Nobody loves your brand as much as you do. We can change that." That really is the goal.

You hope that the people who lead these organizations are ultimately in love with their brands. That's great. But they also have to be impartial and open to hearing the good, the bad, and the ugly about the brand. For example, I look at my daughter and I am just in love with her. I think she is amazing, incredibly beautiful, smart, and talented, but I probably overlook a lot of flaws because she is mine. I made her. She came from my genes and my loins. A brand can be like that, too. It's easy not to see the flaws, especially for founders and long-time team members.

But bringing in an outside brand consultant is getting ahead of ourselves. First, go back and really study the questions in chapters three, four, and five of this book. Dig really deep and answer those questions about your brand. Then take the results and compare them to your current brand strategy. Do they match up? If so, that's great. If not, then you have some work to do. Either way, having the knowledge contained in these pages will put you way ahead of the competition in understanding the true meaning of branding and why it's so important to your future success.

 **INTERVIEW**

WITH CHRISTINE KARPINSKI, REAL ESTATE INVESTOR AND
ENTREPRENEUR, HOWTORENTBYOWNER.COM

### Can you tell us about your business?

I'm a real estate investor who specializes in vacation rental properties. I also own a vacation rental management company. I've written books on the topic and have done a lot of speaking engagements during my 20-year career in this industry. I also spent a fair number of years working at HomeAway.com, which is the leading company for vacation rentals globally. All of this has created the "Christine Karpinski" brand as the industry leader in knowledge and advice.

### How did you first meet Deb Gabor?

Deb and I met when she was doing due diligence for HomeAway before that company really even started. She was conducting market research on the industry and doing due diligence on companies that the founders and investors were considering purchasing. She called upon me as an industry expert for my insights and advice. During that process, the HomeAway CEO, Brian Sharples, realized that I had a lot of industry knowledge that he could utilize. He wanted me to come and work for the company, but I was independent and didn't want to be an employee or jeopardize the brand I had worked so long and hard to create. Ultimately, we structured a deal in a way that I could maintain my independence while working for the company, which is, admittedly, very unusual. Generally, when you go work as an employee, you have to give up your personal brand. But HomeAway recognized I was a valuable asset, and we were able to structure an unconventional deal. Bottom line: if you create a strong enough brand, it'll carry you through!

**Can you tell us a little bit about your branding experience?**
I approached branding from a very unconventional side of things in that I really created my brand around me and my own name, rather than around a business or a product. Maintaining that brand has always been somewhat of a challenge; especially when I worked for HomeAway, because I was constantly straddling the line between working for the company and working for my own brand. Though it's been somewhat of a challenge, it's something I've always been able to maintain.

**Is it true that branding never ends? That it's not just something you do for six months and then you're done?**
Definitely. Deb is really smart about this. I think that's one of the big mistakes companies make. When you're creating a brand there's all the excitement that goes around it. Then once you finally come up with the brand, your brand strategy, all your logos, all your taglines and all of that, then you're like, "Okay. I'm done." That's *not* how it works.

I mean it's very similar to raising a child. You can't just give birth to a child and then expect that it's just going to grow up all on its own. It has to be cared for constantly. The same is true with branding. It's really important for you to nurture your brand and care for it and, of course, make changes as time progresses and stay with it.

**Does branding change over time?**

Yes it can. Just as you have different strategies with your children when they're infants than you do when they're 12 and when they're 20. I think you need to always carry that branding through, because markets change, competitors come and go. As I said before, I think this is a big mistake that especially entrepreneurs make. Remember, you have to continue to maintain it, keep it current, and, most importantly, keep it forefront with your marketing and PR. I am a huge advocate of PR. But with news cycles today, that takes a lot of effort and ongoing work too.

**What happens if a product doesn't deliver on what's promised by the company's brand messaging?**

It's overselling and underdelivering. Sales and Marketing 101, right? You want to do the opposite; you want to undersell and overdeliver. Most entrepreneurs have made this mistake once in their career—and mind you, they only make that mistake once. It's way more work to backpedal on something you've oversold and underdelivered than the other way around.

**Is it important for marketing and branding executives, and even CEOs, to talk to customers regularly?**

OMG! Yes! I think it's really important. Again, this is something that Deb is spot on with. A lot of times the CEO of the company gets buried in the numbers with his or her top priority being the share price and/or pleasing the investors. When they get singularly focused on the numbers, they often lose touch with the customers. If you don't remember who your customer is, if you divert your focus off the customer and servicing that customer, then more often than not that's a clear path to failure. My mantra in business has always been the brand, the product, and the customers always come before the money. While they're not mutually exclusive, often people focus more on the money than anything else. If your focus is only on the money, I say nine times out of 10 you're going to fail.

*CONCLUSION*

# THE POWER OF STORIES

**HUMANS LOVE STORIES**. We *remember* stories. We don't remember features or specs or numbers very well, but we recall good stories. For example, you probably don't remember the number of your first college dorm room. And unless you're Rain Man, you likely don't even remember the address or phone number of the front desk. But I guarantee you could tell at least a dozen very detailed stories about what happened there.

Humans also use stories as a means of identifying and characterizing other people and events. I see this in the dating world a lot. My girlfriends can't remember the *names* of the guys they went out on dates with, but they remember the guys and the dates because of stories about what happened on the date. "Have you heard from had-to-blow-into-a-breathalyzer-to-start-his-car guy lately?" "Guess who I ran into the other day? Refused-to-pay-for-valet guy." "I got the strangest e-mail today from still-lives-with-his-mom guy."

Stories have been around since long before the beginning of recorded history. Researchers have found evidence of stories that date back to the cave men. I took a class in college about the history of the religions of ancient Israel. We studied the Mesopotamian creation epic and the Canaanite creation epic and Genesis from the Old Testament. We studied all of these ancient writings. Thousands of years ago, humans recognized the power of good stories to influence behavior.

The innate fondness and affinity that humans have for stories is what makes branding possible. And it's another reason you should not build your branding around product features and specifications. The strength of your brand comes down to the power of the story you tell.

The strongest brands tell good stories about both the brand and about the customers who use it. Remember, that story is the story of your brand *and* the story that the customers are trying to tell about *themselves*. Brands that do this exceptionally well are the ones that create an emotional bond and irrational loyalty. That emotional bond comes from the story, not from functional things about your product.

By now you're familiar with the key messages of this book. Brand early. Brand often. Brand always. Branding must be ongoing and it's not optional. Brand or be branded. That is the call to action.

Some readers might be overwhelmed by this notion that branding must be ongoing in perpetuity. That can be a lot to swallow. It's kind of like when you get a prescription for some medication and you ask the doctor, "How long do I have to take this?"

The doctor says, "You have to take this every day for the rest of your life if you want to maintain a great quality of life." And so it is with branding. If you stop taking your meds, bad things can happen.

The good news is this is natural. Even though it may seem like a lot to deal with at first, humans are naturally inclined to tell stories. With a little practice, I promise you will become good at this. As a steward of the brand, it's your job to craft your story, to monitor how your audience receives your story, and to adjust your story as needed.

And there's more good news. This ongoing branding process can actually be very personally and professionally fulfilling. It gets you out of your spreadsheets and your production schedules and your product lines, and turns you into a creative storyteller. It allows you to put a compelling brand story out in the marketplace and watch it thrive. I derive tremendous satisfaction from watching my clients' brands succeed and grow and build shareholder value, and I know they do too.

Humans have a deep need to feel connected. Branding is an outlet for that need. The process of talking to customers who love your brand and are deeply emotionally connected to it is uniquely satisfying. The employees and vendors and sales channels that sell your brand all derive success out of your brand story. That, too, can be very fulfilling. A rising tide lifts all boats. Branding done well is the equivalent of finding self actualization in your business.

## I CAN'T NOT BRAND

As I stated in the introduction to this book, I am compelled to share this information. I can't not brand. I feel like I'm going to jump out of my seat if I can't talk about brands with other business people. My passion is to help other people to be successful in their businesses. Speaking in front of people is something that helps me get this information out there. The content in this book is an expanded and far more detailed version of what I speak about.

People ask me all the time, "How do you feel about giving these strategies away and showing other people the tools it took you decades to perfect?" I don't think of these strategies as something I should hoard or keep secret. This is how I'm giving back to a business world that's been incredibly generous and gracious to me. If I can help 100 brands through my consulting practice, or 10,000 brands through this book, I'd rather help the 10,000. Actually, truth be told, I'd rather do both, and I can do both.

So I suggest you read this book from cover to cover, several times. Then implement the tactics and strategies discussed in these pages. My hope and desire is that you will use this book to build a world-class brand with a long life that supports hundreds of jobs up and down your supply chain and distribution channels. And please drop me an e-mail with any questions or just to share your success stories. I really hope to hear from you. Good luck and good branding! Feel free to e-mail me at deb@solmarketing.com or submit a success story or ask a question at BrandingIsSex.com.

*THE END*

# ONE FINAL BONUS TIP

## THE ANTI-ELEVATOR PITCH

See? I told you I can't stop branding. This book ended 20 words ago, and I'm still branding! So here's one final branding tip. I call it the anti-elevator pitch. You are no doubt aware of the concept of the elevator pitch. It's a methodology for getting your point across in the span of an elevator ride—maybe 20 or 30 seconds. Most people look at the elevator pitch as a one-way delivery system for information in which you basically just unload and talk extemporaneously to a captive audience.

I think there is a better way. An elevator pitch should serve as an ask for permission to have a conversation. For instance, I give you a quick teaser statement or ask a provocative question that highlights a problem in need of a solution to get you interested. Then you're so interested in what comes next that you give me permission to go on and tell you more.

I'm an investor in a lot of early-stage technology companies through my InvestorPitches.com business. Believe me, I am on the receiving end of a lot of elevator pitches, most of which fall flat. However, the best elevator pitch I ever heard came from a person from one of these startups. He totally hooked me with a power question: "Deb, what if I told you, you never had to search for another e-mail again?" I saw myself in both the problem (an e-mail inbox with over 8,000 unread messages that I have to search through every time I need to be reminded about a meeting I agreed to attend or a phone number someone sent me) and the solution (never having to plow through that mess again).

In that one statement, he had my attention. I said, "Okay, I don't know *what* your company makes, but I want one." Basically, what his company created was an algorithm that assesses the importance of information in your e-mail and presents it to you in dashboard form. Yawwwwnnnnn.

What he was proposing is what Gmail does today. However, had he come in with a more traditional elevator pitch approach and said, "I'm the founder of this startup. I used to work at Goldman Sachs and I got a lot of e-mails and it was really hard for me to make sense of the ones that were important, not important, whatever." All I would have heard is, "Blah, blah, blah." I probably wouldn't have taken the meeting.

So the anti-elevator pitch is essentially just a better way of storytelling. A good story always hooks the listener right from the start. I learned that from the Whole Foods story-time storytellers in Austin. They would always draw in the listeners within the first 20 seconds. This is also common in fiction books. Just read the opening scene of Dan Brown's gazillion-copy-selling book *The DaVinci Code* for a good example of a great hook.

The anti-elevator pitch is also effective because it starts with why, not what. You want to simply and succinctly tell the story of your company by focusing on *why* you're doing it versus *what* you're doing. When we tell stories, we have a tendency to start with *what* we're doing. But that's backward. As I mentioned earlier, Simon Sinek's "Start with Why" TED Talk is a must-see that is a beautiful introduction to this concept. I highly recommend you watch this. The lesson of this video is the idea that you should communicate your story from a place of passion and explain *why* you're doing something. We actually use the "Start with Why" methodology with branding clients.

So in your anti-elevator pitch, start with an emotional hook that immediately involves and invests your listener in the story. Get the listener's attention, and then get permission to continue. Then go into your elevator pitch. I promise this will work 10 times better than the old way. Heck, the anti-elevator pitch is worth the price of this book by itself, and I put it on the last page.

You're welcome.

# ACKNOWLEDGMENTS

I would like to express my gratitude to all the people who supported me in this journey of writing *Branding Is Sex*. I'd like to thank my friends and biggest fans, Lisa and Cliff Sharples, without whom there probably wouldn't even be a Sol Marketing. I'd also like to thank the current Sol Marketing team—Alexis, Angela, Dana, Max, Rose, Sara, Shaina, and Tansey—for their patience during the distracting process of writing this book.

Additionally, heartfelt thanks go out to Chris Balish, who tirelessly listened to me drone on about what seemed like every lesson I've learned about branding in the past 25 years. Thank you to Tucker Max, for showing me a vision for how my ideas could become a great book.

I would also like to thank the many brands who have contributed to this book by inspiring the desire in me to get their customers laid.

For her dedication to the pursuit of proper punctuation and bringing all my worst ideas to fruition, Lynn Schwartz.

Finally, I'd like to thank my daughter, Hannah McEvilly, who is just everything.

# ABOUT THE AUTHOR

 **DEB GABOR** was born to brand. She is the founder of Sol Marketing, a brand strategy consultancy obsessed with building winning brands. Since 2003, the Sol Marketing team has led brand strategy engagements for household names like Dell, Microsoft, and NBC Universal and digital winners like Allrecipes, Cheezburger, HomeAway, and others. Through Sol Marketing's InvestorPitches.com division, hundreds of startups have benefited from Deb's wizardry for crafting pitches that have raised funding rounds up to $85 million. A displaced Midwesterner, Deb lives in Austin, Texas, land of 300-plus sunny days and the best barbecue west of the Mississippi. Reach Deb at SolMarketing.com and InvestorPitches.com